W9-BHA-648

Reiki
with Gemstones

Ursula Klinger-Omenka

Reiki with Gemstones

Activating Your Self-Healing Powers
Connecting the Universal Life Force Energy
with Gemstone Therapy

LOTUS LIGHT
SHANGRI-LA

The healing applications described in this book originated from the author's own practical experiences. However, they are in no way meant as a substitute for medical advice and help. The author and the publisher do not assume any type of liability for damages that result through the proper or improper use of the methods presented here.

1st American Edition 1997
© by Lotus Light Publications
Box 325
Twin Lakes, WI 53181, USA
The Shangri-La Series is published in cooperation
with Schneelöwe Verlagsberatung, Federal Republic of Germany
© 1990 by Windpferd Verlagsgesellschaft mbH, Aitrang, Germany
All rights reserved
Translated by Christine M. Grimm
Cover design: Monika Jünemann, based on an illustration by Peter Ehrhardt
Interior illustrated: Peter Ehrhardt
ISBN 0-914955-29-2
Library of Congress Catalog Number 97-71448

Printed in the USA

*This book is dedicated to the
increasing large Reiki family and
friends of the precious stones and
crystals with all my love, joy,
and gratitude for my many helpers
in the light world and on earth.*

Table of Contents

Preface

My Personal Path

Many years ago, both of these powers came to me through initiation and have merged into a strong unity that has opened me up to standing with both feet on the earth and made my heart and senses receptive to the experience of wonderful, universal love and light from the divine source.

Reiki has led me to mastery with myself, my surrounding world, and the universal life energy; the gemstones and crystals have guided me to the development of beauty and joy, concentration, and essence in my life. And I have learned to put this power to use in my daily life.

A giant step on my path to Reiki was my difficult pregnancy and the painful and sorrowful experience of letting go of and giving birth to a dead child. In coping with this incisive experience, I discovered my own spirituality. Three years later, in my reincarnation therapy and training I found my way to the universal, divine stream of light and its great liberating, healing power. Shortly thereafter, in the summer of 1983, this key experience led me to Reiki and my First Degree Reiki initiation. Even today, I am filled with much gratitude for my Reiki Master Brigitte Müller, at the time the only Reiki Master living in Germany, through whom I was allowed to receive the gift of Reiki.

A new period of my life began with my Reiki initiation. Reiki gave, and still gives me, the complete certainty of being a channel for light, universal love, and the healing divine power through the initiation, which I receive in complete naturalness, obviousness, and simplicity. All I have to do is lay on my hands, without having to make an effort or visualize anything or fulfill certain rituals or conditions, without excessive demands on my attention while giving Reiki. My hands are always with me, ready to give Reiki. In this process, Reiki always flows optimally on its own to the recipient, as he needs it and is able to accept it, completely independent of my person. This gives me the basis for supporting other people with Reiki, activating their powers of self-healing, examining and renewing their ways of thinking and attitude towards life, as well as their behavior, and expanding and increasing their state of consciousness. One month after my Reiki initiation into the First Degree, I opened the *Institute for Holistic Psychology* and have worked independently with individuals and groups on the basis of Reiki since then.

One year later, in the summer of 1984, I had an unexpected, yet very impressive encounter with a shaman in which the inner experience of the "fire of the earth" threw me to the floor and a tiny black gemstone with white spots came to me, a snowflake obsidian. The shaman gave it to me with the exhortation to listen to what this stone has to say. At that moment, an entirely new dimension opened up within me; gemstones and crystals began to speak to me. Without any previous awareness of it, the "guardian of the stones" came into my consciousness as a superior, divine consciousness of the gemstone world for the first time as I laid gemstones and crystals into a manPala, giving me the initial insights and instructions in dealing with the wonderful color vibrations of the stones. I felt this to be a deep, inner initiation and introduction to the light- filled, mysterious world that had been completely concealed from me up to that time, permitting me to become so intimately connected with the light vibrations and emanations of the gemstones and crystals that I experience them as a part of myself since that time.

On the basis of Reiki, I learned to include the gemstones in my Reiki work through inner guidance. This intensified my energy greatly and further opened me up to Reiki. During the very same year, I was initiated into Second Degree Reiki, which lifted my consciousness, as well as my approach to Reiki and the gemstones, into new areas of existence and possibilities of application. As a result, I have developed my conscious perception of the energetic events and processes within the energy bodies of other human beings, including their auras and energy centers. In addition, my own mediumism, through which I experience what stone is capable of supporting a person in his current life situation, has also become intensified. The gemstone guides my perception in this process. With its emanation, which I can clearly see, it gives me concrete information and help. Through this I learn which vibrations of the soul seek expression.

Time and again, the work with Reiki and gemstones has led me to the latent abilities and potentials concealed within me, bringing them to the "light", meaning consciousness. The angels, very specifically the four archangels and the gemstone and crystal angels, came into my life and work in this way. Since my initiation as a Reiki Master, the ascended masters and the high bearers of light, who constantly direct the great rays of color from the divine source into our stream of life, have also come to me.

During my many experiences with Reiki and gemstones, with myself as well as in the application and initiation of both powers for others, I have let myself be guided by the spiritual world. I express the essence of these experiences here in this book. The special thing about Reiki with gemstones is the natural and direct merging of both powers, which activate and intensify each other as a result, creating more than just the sum of these two energies.

Introduction

Two Natural Powers

Luminous, radiant powers of the universe are concealed in gemstones and crystals, which activate our powers of self-healing in a natural way and help develop our divine light consciousness. With Reiki, a method of (self-)healing rediscovered in Japan, we can channel these luminous, radiant powers of the universe and let them flow into ourselves and others by the laying on of hands. When we use both of these powers for our benefit in combination with each other, complementing and intensifying each other, we are permitted to have wonderful experiences.

The world of gemstones was formed deep within the earth, in Mother Earth's womb. Under enormous pressure and over an inconceivable period of time, they have grown in complete stillness like bright blossoms in the darkness. They contain within them the divine light in its perfection, purity, clarity, and variety. The colors, forms, and structures are displayed in a uniquely concentrated manner, as in no other comparable earthly form of manifestation. The unity of Heavenly Father (light, spirit) and Mother Earth (darkness, matter) is expressed by every gemstone and crystal in a perfect way.

Although we can see and enjoy the beauty, the sparkle, the color intensity, and the form of a gemstone with our "outer eyes" alone, only our "inner eye" is permitted to perceive its concealed powers, its shining and sparkling far out into the universe, its connection to the light world from which it and we ourselves and all life has been created, its need to find us, be accepted and loved, and direct our consciousness to the divine, to light, and to the spirit in matter.

The word Reiki comes from Japanese and is an expression of the universal life energy, which was rediscovered by a Christian priest who lived and taught in Japan, Dr. Mikao Usui, during the 19th century as the divine, universal healing power with which Buddha and Christ had healed through the laying-on of hands. It is the power that flows to us from the source of Eternal Light, pours through us, and surrounds us. This power is available in abundance and could actually be put to use by each of us.

However, as a result of our physical bodies alone after entering this life we are bound to the solid vibrations of matter, earthly processes, and the resulting needs, still far removed from the rediscovery of our light home. Yet, with the increasing development of our light consciousness, we are allowed to once again recognize the correlations between matter and spirit. Then our souls' longing and striving to return to its source, to the light, to the divine, becomes stronger and stronger and so intense that the light can flow to us with increasing vigor and force.

There are many possibilities for activating our light vibrations in such a way that we can open up to the light of life, the universal life energy, and thereby allow the healing, divine ray of light with its unconditional love to increasingly flow to us.

One of the possibilities for being strongly connected with the universal life energy is the initiation into Reiki. With this initiation, our healing channels are cleansed and activated in such a way that we become a mediator between spirit and matter in a simple and natural way. This life energy flows on its own through initiated Reiki hands whenever we are willing for it to do this, going wherever we place them.

Both Reiki and gemstones are natural, strong, and concentrated light forces that awaken the divine light consciousness within us to new liveliness.

The Creation of Gemstones from the Inner, Spiritual Perspective

Even long before the Earth became visible, an idea and a plan of creation for the realization of this idea had originated in the world of light. Many different color rays and light beings connected with this color ray formed themselves from the unity of the light. Every color ray and each light being makes sure that they can express themselves in accordance with their vibration on the material level. The light beings of gemstones concealed their manifestations deep in the darkness of the earth, not visible to those whose attentiveness doesn't reach far enough into the depths. These light beings constantly accompanied the creation and growth of their stone in the womb of the earth, helped it survive the immense pressure situations, gave it some of their luminous color, and concentrated it in an endlessly slow process of growth. And they made sure that it became the image of their vibration: an expression of their light, their spiritual, subtle state of being, embedded in the conditions and possibilities, structures, forms and colors of the solid vibrations, which means of the earth.

Full of trust and love, conscious of their luminous beauty in the hidden places, the light beings wait, sometimes for millions and thousands of years, until their manifestations, the gemstones, are discovered by human beings. They help Mother Earth and her "stone children" to survive the violent process of extracting them and removing them from the womb of the earth with hammer and spike, with blasting, or with power shovels. When a stone is cut, the angels also feel themselves attracted to this process of refinement, which increases consciousness, and accompany this process of emphasizing and perfecting the beauty of the stone.

In this way, the light beings are also prepared to find access to our consciousness. In all cultures and religions, gemstones and crystals have experienced special respect that increased their "standing" by not only regarding them as jewelry, decoration, or valuable objects, but also as bearers of power, charms, talismans, etc. Particularly in recent years, many people have become more open, receptive, and prepared for the concealed powers, the subtle vibrations of the gemstones than ever before. Because of this, a great many light beings and angels of gemstones are now being rewarded for their long waiting and find their way to their light work on earth through human beings and the more intensely developing light consciousness of human beings.

With each gemstone and crystal that I hold in my hand, I become more aware of this wonder of creation: I am in contact with a piece of eternity, with light powers that have waited for me for hundreds, thousands, or even millions of years.

Today there are a great many instructions and teachings on the possibilities of coming into contact with the light powers of the stones and perceiving and using their vibrations for healing and development of consciousness. I will show how the light powers of the gemstones and crystals can be activated through Reiki in a totally natural way—a very special possibility—in this book.

Reiki
Source and Rediscovery

The powers of Reiki came from the same source as those of the gemstones and their powers of light. All of life itself comes from this source: divine light. A divine spark from this original sea of light and love has remained in the consciousness of the human being, striving to become a channel of light for the healing and fulfilling all-embracing love of the universal life energy. Human beings also were initially designed as an idea in the spiritual plan of Creation and then created in the image of God with the "Higher Self." The Higher Self of a human being is always in the world of light and accompanies and guides the person, directing him towards the light time and again through all the incarnations and during all of his experiences. As long as we do not recognize the light, seeing only with our "outer" eyes in the material world, we are also far removed from our source, the divine power of love, just like the gemstones in the darkness of the earth. But through the connection with our Higher Self, which has already accompanied our soul through many incarnations and "shaping processes" in all of life on earth, we receive opportunities over and over for more consciously finding the light.

In a direct and very special way, we can come into contact with our Higher Self and beyond with the universal life energy, the original sea of light: through the channel of light, which we also call the healing channel.

However, we have blocked this light channel through our actions, thoughts, and feelings. Only when we increasingly turn to divine consciousness and the growing desire for unity, harmony, and healing are the light vibrations activated that make it possible for the divine, universal light energy to flow to us. The channel is opened once again.

All religions and high cultures are concerned with the human being turning to the light, the reunification with this life-giving, healing, all-embracing love, with the unity with God. All founders of religions have realized this unity and have given their "students" help in also finding this path. It is a primary desire of our soul to return back to the light home. Individual souls that have developed particular strength in this light consciousness incarnate time and again on earth in order to support people in finding their way out of unconsciousness, thereby helping others as well.

The discovery of Reiki is also based on this longing of the soul for reunification with the divine light and its universal healing love.

At the end of the 19th century, a priest by the name of Mikao Usui lived and taught in Japan. He was the head of a small Christian university in Kyoto. When asked by one of his oldest students whether he knew how Jesus healed, he could not answer this question. It became a challenge for him. He resigned his office as head of the Doshisha University and set out to search for an answer. At first, he travelled to the USA and was awarded the doctor's degree in ancient languages, in which he searched to decipher the secret. He didn't find it here and returned to Japan when he became aware that there were also reports of the healing power of Buddha and his students in the tradition of Buddhism. He visited various monasteries, studied Japanese translations of Buddhist writings, and learned Chinese in order to attain an even greater overview of the Buddhist writings. But only when he decided to learn Sanskrit, the language of the oldest Buddhist writings, was he led to notes by one of Buddha's students: descriptions, formulas, and symbols related to how Buddha had healed. After seven years, Dr. Usui had found what he had been looking for. However, his knowledge of the symbols wasn't enough to bring him into contact with the healing spiritual power. He followed the advice of an old friend, an abbot, fasting and meditating for 21 days on one of Japan's holy mountains. Finally, on the 21st day, a tremendous beam of light came down from the heavens to him. Had he followed his initial impulse, he would have preferred to run away from it. Yet, he suddenly knew that this was exactly what he had been waiting for.

He was touched by this light and experienced a changed state of consciousness. As he sank to the ground, Dr. Usui saw a quick succession of light bubbles containing the symbols he had uncovered in his studies. These symbols burned themselves solidly into his consciousness and revealed themselves to him as the key to divine healing power.

Dr. Usui called this rediscovered power, with which Buddha and Jesus had already healing by the laying on of hands, Reiki. This is the Japanese expression for universal life energy. He founded the Usui System of Natural healing, gave many people Reiki, and taught those who wanted to know more about this power how to use Reiki. He also taught them to heal themselves, to change their lives with the Reiki life principles that he had written, and thereby find an improved attitude towards life.

Up to this day, Reiki is traditionally only passed on and taught through initiations by a Reiki Master.

Before his crossing into the spiritual world, Dr. Usui appointed a student who was deeply dedicated to him and to Reiki, Dr. Chujiro Hayashi, a retired marine officer, to become his successor, to become a *Master of Reiki*, and entrusted him with the *Essence of Reiki*.

Dr. Hayashi founded a Reiki clinic in Kyoto and Tokyo, to which a Japanese woman who lived on Hawaii, Hawayo Takata, also came with a tumor disease in 1935. She was healed through Reiki and became a Reiki channel herself. She remained for one year to train at the clinic, thereafter returning to Hawaii, where she practiced Reiki. In 1937, Dr. Hayashi visited her for several months and gave her further training. Before his departure in February of 1938, he initiated her to

18

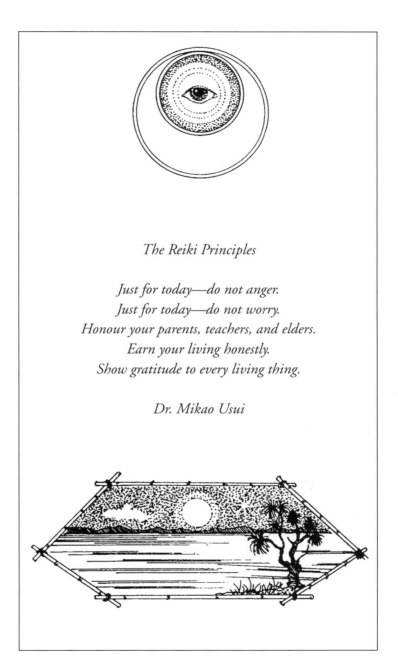

The Reiki Principles

Just for today—do not anger.
Just for today—do not worry.
Honour your parents, teachers, and elders.
Earn your living honestly.
Show gratitude to every living thing.

Dr. Mikao Usui

be the first and, at that time, only authorized person in the USA to become a *Master of the Dr. Usui Reiki System of Healing.*

Before the outbreak of the war between the USA and Japan, he passed on the Essence of Reiki to Hawayo Takata in Japan, giving her both the title of "Master of Reiki" and the authorization to be his successor. He then left his body in the circle of his family and the Reiki Masters who taught in Japan.

Reiki became known in the West through Hawayo Takata. She initiated and trained 21 Reiki Masters, among them Phyllis Lei Furumoto, her granddaughter who she had already initiated into Reiki during childhood. However, only in the year 1979, after college and career, was Phyllis Lei Furumoto prepared to be initiated as a Master and be intensively instructed and trained in Reiki. When Hawayo Takata made hitransition in December 1980, it was clear that Phyllis Lei Furumoto was to be her successor in the Reiki lineage. She gave her the title *Master of Reiki* and the Essence of Reiki. Since that time, Phyllis Lei Furumoto bears the responsibility for Reiki. Many Masters have been initiated by her and other Reiki Masters in the meantime so that there are now currently several thousands who initiate and teach throughout the entire world. And the Reiki family is continually growing, letting us here on earth be joined in light and love, just as we have long been in the spiritual world.

Initiation into Reiki

Reiki's special quality is the cleansing and activating of the healing channel through the ceremony of *initiation* and the simplicity of its application by the *laying on of hands*.

The Reiki initiation can only be given through a Reiki Master. For this purpose, he uses the symbols and mantras that Dr. Usui rediscovered. These are passed on from Master to Master.

Alone the desire to become a healing channel for yourself or for others is enough to put you into the vibration that leads to Reiki. Anyone who comes to the Reiki initiation is inwardly, more or less consciously, willing and prepared to receive Reiki. With his personal emination, he is guided to people and/or writings* that have sensitized his consciousness for Reiki.

The initiation into Reiki supports, strengthens, and confirms the direct, powerful, and concentrated connection with the universal life energy. It lets us become a channel, mediator, and transformer of this spiritual healing power so that it can be received and used on all levels, mind, soul, and body. And this occurs in the way needed by the recipient and signaled directly, clearly, and unmistakably to the universe through his emination.

Based on the tradition, Reiki is passed on and taught in two degrees through initiation.

---

* Also see: Paula Horan, Reiki Master: *Abundance Through Reiki* and Bodo J. Baginski/ Shalila Sharamon: *Reiki—Universal Life Energy.*

Reiki Initiation into the First Degree

With the initiation through a Reiki Master into First Degree Reiki, the initiated person is brought into connection with the universal life energy, the light of life, through four consecutive attunement: through the cleansing and activation of his healing channel. At the same time, this brings with it an intensive flooding of light to the physical body and its energy system. An extensive cleansing lasting for 21 days, permeates our body in this process; old pain and suffering can resurface as a healing reaction and challenge us to give ourselves a great deal of Reiki. However, blocks and fears can also appear during this special cleansing phase. They come into the "light" again, because of Reiki and bring with them a new confrontation with our modes of behavior.

Even with the First Reiki Degree, the person initiated into Reiki is in contact strongly with the universal life energy through his specially activated healing channel, and Reiki flows powerfully through his initiated hands.

Reiki flows on its own wherever a Reiki channel, which is what a person initiated into Reiki is often called, puts his hands. This happens in the way needed by the recipient, who attracts it through his own vibrations.

Together with the initiation, the Reiki student also receives instructions in the application of Reiki and how he can lay on his hands for himself or for others in order to make possible an optimal flow of Reiki. He will become increasingly familiar with how to deal with this force in a natural and simple manner. The Reiki hand positions are no secret and can be used by anyone, even without Reiki initiation. However, this should not be mistaken for Reiki and is also not substitute for the initiation into Reiki, which brings the healing channel and the energy level of the initiated person into a lasting vibration of light. This vibration of light allows the healing, divine flow of energy to stream through the hands in a natural way at any time on its own, without any effort, without a person having to visualize, activate, or maintain inner images or ideas.

With the initiation, the Reiki student learns that he is "just" a channel for Reiki, for the universal life energy that flows through him from the highest divine source: for himself or others. At the same time, we do not determine the effect this power should have with our limited minds, but instead leave this up to the highest guidance. Full of trust and in the knowledge that it flows into the areas where it is needed in precisely the required intensity, we are only its channel.

Reiki Initiation into the Second Degree

The initiation into the Second Reiki Degree takes place through a Reiki Master, who mentally prepares the students and gives them the Reiki symbols in the form discovered, taught, and passed on by Dr. Usui and trains them in their application. This initiation intensifies the connection with Reiki and increases the vibrations of light in our healing channels and in each of our energy bodies. The aura of a Reiki student initiated into the Second Degree therefore becomes much stronger and more concentrated in its vibration of light. This initiation is also followed by 21 days of cleansing. This promotes an intense confrontation with ourselves in accordance with the strong flooding of light in all of our energy bodies: our concepts of self, expectations, and ideals, rigid modes and patterns of behavior, hurt feelings and burdening habits in life.

Because of the increased light vibrations in the healing channel and in all of our energy bodies, as well as the use of the symbols, Reiki flows in a much more concentrated manner through the Reiki channel. Spiritual development, as well as the realisation and development of mental perceptions and powers in daily life is thereby intensified and accelerated. At the same time, it is possible for the student of the Second Degree to open up to new dimensions of divine being through the increased light vibrations in his Reiki channel and use of the symbols. This makes it possible to intensify the universal life energy at any given place into a more concentrated form, raise unconscious processes more intensely into consciousness, give mental and distance healings, greet the divine in its forms of appearance and manifestation, and send Reiki into a situation, a room, a meeting, an experience, a person, a stone, an animal, a plant, a light being, an angel, a Higher Self... There is an inexhaustible potential here because, no matter how we feel at the moment or what we are doing, we can always send out Reiki. When we give Reiki directly through the laying on of hands, we also do not determine what effect Reiki should have in the recipient but simply make this power available to him in the trust and knowledge that the divine wisdom in Reiki and the recipient best knows what should be supported with Reiki.

In a natural way through the laying on of hands and/or the concentration of the universal life energy, the initiations into Reiki create a basis for being a channel. Whatever develops from the basis of this foundation is then completely dependent on the Reiki application. Each person initiated into Reiki bears the responsibility for this himself. It is also up to him whether these gifts are left fallow or whether he permits their growth.

The Connection Between Reiki and Gemstones

Gemstones are living, pulsating vibrations, even if they appear rigid and lifeless to us. Their vibrations are, in accordance with their appearance and composition, very color-intensive, concentrated, and created precisely in structures, patterns, and forms. If we want to touch and activate the subtle light powers of the gemstones and crystals, directing them to ourselves, we must greet them with light and love. As a result, we intensify their light-filled emanation. We can do this in various ways such as rituals, visualizations, and programming. A very powerful, simple, natural, and concentrated activation of the light energies of gemstones occurs through Reiki.

Our initiated Reiki hands radiate very intensive light and love whenever they touch something in this consciousness. When, as a Reiki channel, we pick up a gemstone, it immediately feels that it is loved, accepted, and flooded with light and love. It can immediately develop its divine shine and glow in this light activation and find a heartfelt access to us.

It is wonderful for a gemstone to be touched with Reiki. Its luminous, brilliant color vibrations extend far out into the universe, in the great energy stream of its color ray. Here it is lovingly received by *its* light being. The gemstone has achieved its highest fulfillment when it has found a human being who permits it to ascend through his light-consciousness and again become one with the spiritual world. The joy of reunification in the light is great. Its gratitude to the person who has made this "homecoming" possible through his light channel, through Reiki, is also great, and the blessing that comes back to the earth and the one giving the Reiki, as well as the recipient, is also infinitely loving and beneficial as a result.

When the light vibrations in our Reiki channel, our energy bodies, and our hands are increased even more and concentrated through initiation into the Second Degree, we can boost the stone's light power and thereby also the intensity of its shine and emanation, meaning its effect, through the use of the symbols. We receive an intuitive message from the stone, come into contact with the divine being of the stone, and merge with it.

When a gemstone is greeted, activated, and strengthened through the symbols from a person initiated into the Second Reiki Degree, its vibration can be raised to its highest light being in the great energy stream of its color ray. The regained unity evokes enormous light waves full of joy, liveliness, and beauty. These flood through all the levels down to the earth and leave a blessed "glow" everywhere.

Reiki has a very "enlivening" and light-activating effect on the stone in a simple and natural way. It thereby makes it possible for the stone to develop in accordance with its higher purpose and ascend in its color ray from which it was created through its strongly activated shine and emanation.

If we include gemstones and crystals in Reiki, they strengthen, concentrate, and differentiate the stream of the universal life energy. They direct a portion of the Reiki that flows through us into the area where the stones are laid and stream the very intensive vibration of their brilliant color at this point. At the same time, they make it possible for the light being of this color ray to join in supporting the Reiki-gemstone treatment.

People react very strongly to colors, whether they are aware of it or not. We not only perceive colors through our eyes, but also through our energy centers, which continuously accept and give off subtle vibrations.

These energy centers are taken into particular consideration in the Reiki hand positions: the hands are laid on all of the energy centers one after the other.

If one or more of these energy centers have gemstones put on them when giving Reiki, the concentrated energy (matter) and light emanation of the gemstones becomes concentrated into the transformation of energy. As a result, Reiki is intensified, "attracted," and taken in. Reiki and the brightly shining color vibrations of the gemstones that have been activated are then intensified as they flow together into the energy center beneath the stone that lies under the hands radiating Reiki.

The Selection of Gemstones

Before we give Reiki in connection with the gemstones, we should first turn to the world of gemstones and their color rays and light beings. These are at hand through the presence of the stones in front of us and the Reiki vibrations emanating from us.

Greeting: We greet the gemstones in their beauty and brilliant emanation and for a moment we are conscious that they are a bit of eternity - manifested, living, shining spirit. We thereby acknowledge their divine being, show gratitude that they are there for us, and thank them for their dedication and willingness to help us.

Selection: There are a great many possibilities for selecting gemstones for a Reiki (self-)treatment. Here are some suggestions: We intuitively choose a gemstone and request inner guidance as to where we should place it. Or we lay it on an energy center that particularly needs the color of this stone. When we give Reiki as we do this, the light vibration of the gemstone radiates intensively from the spot where it lays and gently flows from there with the stream of light and love from Reiki into all the areas that need and attract Reiki.

A Special Form

We can also choose a specially cut gemstone such as a ball, an egg, a pyramid, an obelisk, a faceted, convex, or crystallized gemstone.

The light energy of this gemstones is directed into the higher area of one of our energy bodies during the entire Reiki (self-)treatment.

Same Form and Different Types of Stones

We can select a number of gemstones with the same form in various types of stones, such as three pyramids: one of quartz crystal, one of citrine, and one of amethyst. When giving Reiki, we lay them on three different energy centers. In the process, the pyramid energy is activated in the three different aspects. In this particular case, in the *manifestation* of wisdom (quartz crystal), courage and self-confidence (citrine), intuition and spirituality (amethyst). This is further differentiated through the respective energy centers on which the pyramids are located.

One Type of Stone in Various Forms

We can also select a number of gemstones of the same type in various forms; for example, an egg, a ball, a pyramid, and an obelisk of rose quartz. To give Reiki, we could lay the egg on the first, the ball on the third, the pyramid on the sixth, and place the obelisks behind the head on the seventh energy center or between the feet (foot centers). The quality of the rose quartz (blossoming in unconditional love, gentle power that causes resistance and blocks to melt away) flows through the special forms of the gemstone in high, extremely light-filled, pink-colored vibrations into our energy bodies and into the body/gland areas that have a reciprocal action with the respective energy centers.

Nine Stones of Various Colors

We can select nine gemstones of different colors. We lay them on the seven main centers and the two important secondary centers in keeping with their colors. For example, a black-and-white gemstone (snowflake obsidian or tourmaline quartz) can be placed between the feet for activating the foot centers, a red stone (jasper, hematite, garnet, or ruby) on the first energy center, an orange-colored stone (carnelian) on the second energy center, a yellow stone (tiger-eye, amber, pyrite, citrine, precious topaz, or rutile quartz) on the third energy center, a green and a pink-colored stone (chrysocolla, malachite, moss agate, jade, chrysoprase, chrysoberyll, olivine, calcite, emerald, or tourmaline and a rhondonite, rhodochrosite, rose quartz, or kunzite) on the fourth energy center, a light-blue stone (turquoise, larimar, chalcedony, blue precious topaz, or aquamarine) on the fifth energy center, a dark-blue stone (hawk's eye, sodalite, azurite, lapis lazuli, or sapphire) on the sixth energy center, a violet stone (sugilite or amethyst) on the seventh energy center, and a quartz crystal in one hand (hand energy centers).

As a result, each energy center receives stimulation and support of its main function from the corresponding color energy through the gemstone. This activation is both optimal and holistic, cleansing, charging, and harmonizing the energy centers and our entire energy system. It should only take place once a week.*

Seven Gemstones of the Same Type

We select seven gemstones of the same type and lay them on the seven main energy centers for the Reiki treatment. For example, you can use seven garnets or seven carnelians or seven pieces of amber stones or seven citrines or seven olivines or seven chrysoprases or seven emeralds or seven tourmalines or seven aquamarines or seven lapis lazulis or seven sugilites or seven amethysts or seven quartz crystals.

As a result, one aspect of a very special type is activated in each energy center. This aspect is expressed on all levels of our

---

* This is described in great detail in my book *The Secrets of Precious Stones—A Guide to the Activation of the Seven Human Energy Centers Using Gemstones, Crystals and Minerals,* Lotus Light Publications, Wilmot, WI, 1988, pp128.

being to the same degree. For example, the *garnets* with their brilliant red activate joyful initiative and give the body vitality. The *carnelians*, with their softly shimmering orange-colored light bring us "into the flow," flood us with warmth, and increase our feeling for life. *Pieces of ambers* help us permit success in our life. The yellow *citrines* encourage us to translate intuitively perceived truth into practical living and allow wisdom to become alive and visible. *Olivine*, with its green, gives us warmheartedness and kindness. The apple-green shimmering *chrysoprases* give us a natural approach to life's processes of transformation, with development and decay. The intensively bright-green *emeralds* impart universal love and responsibility for ourselves, all creatures, the earth, and the universe. The green-and-pink-colored *tourmaline wands* make it possible for us to break through to unconditional love. The light-blue glowing *aquamarines* release us from emotional entanglements and are balsam for the soul. The dark-blue *lapis lazulis*, often streaked with shimmering gold-colored pyrite, strengthen the soul's great power of faith and give us inner peace. The violet shimmer of *sugilite* helps us become more familiar with the power of our thoughts and feelings, using them meaningfully in divine harmony. The *amethysts* let our drives become the urges for spiritual development and lift our needs to the level of the divine. The *quartz crystals*, which bring us to the light of life, cleanse, clarify, and organize our subtle energies.

This is also the manner of selection described specifically in this book. The instructions on the work with seven of the same gemstones were first "given" to me from the spiritual world when I became a Reiki Master and opened me up to completely new dimensions of the light-filled universe. It is a wonderful experience to be totally flooded with the shining light of a gemstone and have very intensive experiences as a result.

I would like to mention this once again: Before we select a gemstone, we should ask for divine guidance. Impulses, inspirations, and instructions will then arise very spontaneously; we should follow them in all simplicity.

Even if we, for example, have determined right from the start with which gemstones we would like to work, we should continue to let ourselves be guided intuitively as to which type(s) and form(s) would like to accompany us in the Reiki treatment.

When we listen to our higher inner guidance, we can best connect with the momentary situation in life and the individual needs of the person receiving Reiki, further intensifying this effect through the chosen gemstones. For the person selecting the gemstones, this is very good training in letting oneself be guided through trust in one's own intuition.

Effects through the Various Properties of the Gemstones

The intensity and clarity of a gemstone's color, its markings and pattern, size, cut, and form are very important for its effect. The subtle vibrations and entities of a stone correspond precisely with the externally visible manifestations of the gemstone.

The Color

Each color, as well as the many possible nuances of a color, is found in the vibrations of our energy centers, auras, and energy bodies. A gemstone stimulates exactly the color nuances within us that we can see in it. This is why we should be careful not to select any gemstones with dull, cloudy, or dirty colors but choose stones with colors that are clear, pure, and intensive. This will activate the color vibrations within us that have strong cleansing, clarifying, and charging powers.

Opaque, meaning non-transparent gemstones with colors that do not transmit light, bring the energy inside of us into vibrations that are related to earthly embodied solid matter: for example, the black-and-white *snowflake obsidian* roots us within Mother Earth and allows us to perceive and enjoy the beauty that is created through the loving unity with the Heavenly Father. The *red jasper* harmonizes sick, burdensome vibrations of the uterus and ovaries, also functioning as a "midwife." The yellow-brown shimmering *tiger-eye* strengthens the analytical powers of mind that we often need for tests.

The green *malachite* teaches us to accept responsibility for ourselves and no longer give others the "blame" for what happens to us. The pink-black *rhodonite* loving leads us to our shadow side and helps us accept and integrate it into our personality. The light-blue *chalcedony* strengthens our verbal expression. The dark-blue *lapis lazuli* lets our high ideals, our spiritual goals, our connection with our light helpers, as well as our exaggerated self-concept, come to consciousness and take on a livable form. The violet *sugilite* allows us to perceive that the spirt creates the matter and teaches us how to apply the powers of the imagination.

Transparent, translucent, and clear gemstones bring us into lighter vibrations that free our energies from things that burden us, increasing our emanation of light.

The *tourmaline quartz*, with its black tourmaline needles in the light quartz crystal, gives us relief from the tragedy of the soul and dependencies on relationships and earthly, material goods. The *ruby* unites red and blue, matter and spirit, body and soul, sexuality and spirituality, initiative and the power of faith, spontaneity and common sense. The orange rays of the *fire opal* awaken the enthusiasm of our hearts and thereby permit us to be set into more intensive motion, in which we can also "move" others. The *rutile quartz* with its golden rutile needs in the light quartz crystal soothes, harmonizes, and heals the pain that comes from inner conflict, as well as when excessively strong tensions occur. The green *emerald* strengthens us in universal love and opens our consciousness to permitting and accepting love. The pink-colored *kunzite* leads us to the highest level of spiritual love; heart and mind find a unity that liberates us from the "either-or" state. The light-blue *precious topaz* "washes away" hardened, rigid, and outdated modes of behavior and thought patterns in a very gentle way. The dark-blue *sapphire* awakens the soul's great powers of faith and the knowledge about the feeling of security in our cosmic home. The violet *amethyst* strengthens the intuition and leads us on the path to enlightenment.

The pure quartz crystal cleanses, clarifies, and organizes our energies. It gives us objectives, reveals wisdom to us, and unites us with everything in the light.

The *diamond* brings us a perfect consciousness of light and love in all aspects of our existence when it is cut as a brilliant and thereby shines and glows in perfect purity and beauty in all of its facets.

The Markings and Patterns

The markings, patterns, structures, and inclusions of gemstones are just as varied, individual, and unique as those of every human being. If we open up to them on a deeper level, we will find an access to our inner images of the soul through them; feelings and experiences that are within us and want to come back to the light, meaning consciousness, are given life.

This process is so special that there are no generalized instructions as to which markings of a stone evoke certain sensations within a person. The effect is very intensively related to deeply concealed structures of the soul.

The Size

The size of a gemstone alone does not have much to say about its effect. This depends very much on the intensity and purity of the color, whether the stone is cut or not, perfectly whole or damaged, and milky or clear.

A small gemstone, particularly one that is translucent and cut with facets, has the effect of a focus, centering our energy and directing it to what is essential.

A larger gemstone challenges us to overcome feelings of inferiority, narrowness, and pettiness and say "yes" to greatness, vastness, and expansion.

However, if the form, cut, and quality of two gemstones with different sizes closely resemble each other, then the emanation of the larger one is stronger. Yet, it is very important that the person who wears the stone or has it laid on his body during a Reiki treatment is in harmony with the stone's size. This means that the size and radiant power of the vibrations emanating from the stone evokes a response within him.

Cut and Form

Through *uncut gemstones*, we come into contact with our elemental forces, as well as the elemental forces of our environment and those of the spiritual world. The quartz crystals and all the light-filled crystallized parts of a type of stone have a very special meaning in this respect. An example of this is that the rhodochrosite, frequently opaque pink streaked with white lines, also occurs in a very crystalline, translucent, and intensive pink. The azurite, which tends to be a porous stone frequently joined with malachite and chrysocolla, crystallizes in intensively dark-blue shimmering needles that have grown into a ball. The amethyst comes in all the shades of violet, ranging from completely opaque to translucent to totally transparent. This also applies to other stones such as the citrine, topaz, tourmaline, rose quartz, olivine, dioptase, emerald, aquamarine, sapphire, ruby, and diamond. The transparent crystallizations in bright, pure colors bear the *essence* of a gemstone's vibrations within itself, the highest light manifestations and emanations that this type of stone can produce. They connect us with the elemental forces of the light in the large color rays of the universe, which let the luminous color be created out of the unity of pure light from the very beginning. The powers inherent to them are therefore granted to us in the most perfect way.

Cut gemstones have experienced an increase of their energy through their refinement. Rough places, indentations, damage, and so forth have been cut and polished away. The beauty and luminous power of a stone is increased or even first brought to expression through this process. Cut gemstones activate very similar processes within us.

The form in which a stone is cut is very decisive for its area of effectiveness. While the colors have an impact on our energy centers, cleanse us, charge and permeate us, the form directs the energy of the stone more strongly into either the physical, emotional, or mental/spiritual areas.

Tumbled gemstones are, as their name already implies, cut in a drum. Hunks of rock, abrasive, and water are set into motion together so that the stones mutually cut each other.

Through these stones, we come into contact with powers and people who trigger the "friction process" within us. They are a mirror for what we don't (want to) see within ourselves.

Dome-cut gemstones can be found in the **cabochon form** and have a domed surface, a "mountain" above the flat base. They are cut into shapes that are rectangular, oval, drops, round, and fantasy forms. The flat base gives us a good relationship to the earth, and the dome above it has a gentle, feminine energy. The effect of the individual forms corresponds to that of gemstones cut with facets, yet it is much more soft and supportive.

With the *facet cut*, the optical properties of transparent gemstones are emphasized and highlighted by the symmetrical cut of small, smooth, numerous, exact surfaces—the facets. Within the facet cut, there are a great many different varieties. The brilliant cut is very well-known and used for the diamond, as well as other types of transparent gemstones. The facets are very numerous and done in such a way that the light rays flowing into the stone are repeatedly reflected within it before they once again leave with a very intensive radiation. This increases the glow, and the color's sparkling and glittering develops a strong play, the "fire" of the gemstone. This cut kindles our inner fire, lively love, a power that challenges us to the utmost and gives us everything we need to unfold the light within.

Faceted cut gemstones are like a focus that very strongly attracts the light-permeated color energy of its stone from the great color ray of the universe, directing it into our energy system. The form of the surface determines into which channels this intensively vibrating light energy flows:

Rectangular, square forms are the building blocks for the earth. They strengthen the energy occurrence on levels related to the mastering of existence, materialize spiritual vibrations, allow our ideas, inspirations, and intuitions to become visible reality.

Oval forms provide for our physical well-being, for protection and healing of the body, for the satisfaction of our physical needs.

Drop forms unite the rounded, receptive, devoted, supportive feminine with the purposeful masculine that strives for the highest level and activates strong powers of the soul, as well as the mastery of the emotions.

Round forms strengthen the intuitive, inspirational, imaginative, inventive powers of the mind within us and round us off.

The *egg form* activates creative/inventive processes, initiates fresh beginnings, lets new life be created, and makes different experiences possible.

The *triangular form* opens us up to the perception and conscious use of spiritual powers.

The *pyramid* unites four triangles on the basis of the square, which activates the manifesting, material-related energies. The spirit is then merged with matter and the entire energy then directed towards unity, towards the highest plane, to the top where the energies of the four triangles meet. This helps us master the challenges of matter with mental power and fill our life on earth with spiritual strives towards unity in the light.

The *obelisk* stabilizes the pyramid energy, gives us steadfastness in our faith, unshakable trust, and an emanation of light that can be seen from afar, similar to that of a lighthouse.

The *ball* has a rounding effect on ourselves and our picture of the world, bringing confrontations with power and strength, liberating us from strong resistance, concentrating us within our own center, and letting us develop responsibility for ourselves, the earth, and the universe. It brings us to perfection.

With each gemstone that is cut in one of these special forms, with each quartz crystal and with each light-filled crystallized gemstone, we are connected with the light beings who show themselves in the form of angels and communicate with us. With their unending love for us human beings, they can find their way to us if we touch and develop the light powers of the stone in love. They are always willing to support us in lifting our consciousness and our need for love to the light, to strongly accompany us in our "cutting process", and to let our light consciousness become visible and perceptible on the earth.

Cleansing and Activating

Before and after every Reiki treatment with gemstones I both manually and spiritually cleanse the stones selected for this purpose. To do this, hold them under cold, running water for a short time and imagine that everything heavy and dark is being washed away from them.

Afterwards, I dry them with a clean cotton towel and hold them in my Reiki hands. The stones are activated in their light vibrations through the concentrated light energy and the love from the divine, universal source that radiates on its own from our Reiki hands. In this way, the emanations of the gemstones are not only cleansed but also brought into the powerfully healing, harmonizing vibrations that correspond to the energy flow of Reiki.

It is only when they are touched with light and love that the concealed, subtle powers of light are highlighted in the gemstones.

Reiki hands do this on their own in a completely simple and natural way.

During the Reiki treatment, the gemstones experience a strong charging with Reiki. Long after the conclusion of the treatment and after being cleansed, they continue to radiate this Reiki energy within the room or to the person who takes the stone with him. For this reason, we leave the stones with which we have given the Reiki treatments in the room: they provide a beneficial, pure, and lovely atmosphere there. If we have given ourselves a Reiki self-treatment with various gemstones, we can select one of them and carry it with us during the day or even for a longer period of time. It will accompany us with its light. Reiki will have intensified its effect.

Laying the Gemstones and Their Optimal Alignment on the Energy Centers

As the name already says, our energy centers are particularly receptive to subtle light energies: These are bridges over which all of our bodies, from the physical to the cosmic, are in contact and constant exchange of energy with each other. Each energy center has a special task and function in this process, and yet, each bit of information is present and accessible in each of the energy centers.

If we put the gemstone on an energy center, its activating light energy flows into the energy streams of the center. In accordance with the color, form, size, markings, and pattern of the stone, the effect will have certain nuances. We lay the gemstone for the:

1st energy center (base center) on the lower genital area
2nd energy center (sacral center) on the abdomen below the navel
3rd energy center (solar plexus center) above the navel
4th energy center (heart center) between the breasts
5th energy center (throat center) in the hollow of the throat
6th energy center (forehead center) above the bridge of the nose between the eyebrows
7th energy center (head center) behind the head.
The gemstone for the
foot centers is placed between the feet, for the
hand centers on top of the hand facing upwards or under the palm of the hand facing the floor.

Laying the Gemstones and Their Optimal Alignment on the Energy Centers

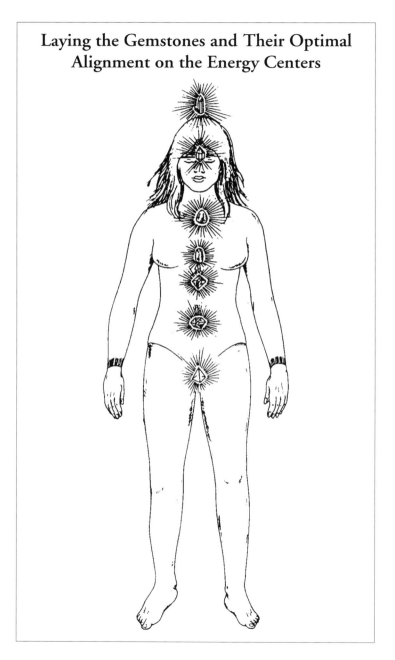

In accordance with the cleansing and activating of the gemstone described above, we laid it on the body and make sure that we align it in the optimal direction. Every gemstone, whether uncut or tumbled, cut in facets or as a cabochon, gives us indications about its energy course through its form, markings, pattern, growth structures, or inclusions. We usually find a tip, a triangle, a mountain, or just a "peak" towards which the energy strives. This is then the area of the stone that should be directed towards the head. This is very clear in quartz crystals or similar stones.

There are two possibilities for optimal alignment when laying out pyramids:

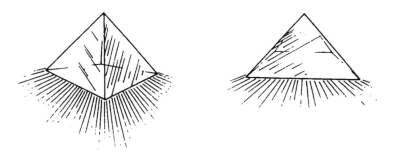

One corner of the pyramid points to the head: the energy flows from the spirit into matter and light energy supports us in earthly occurrences.

One of the base surfaces of the pyramid points to the head: the energy raises itself from the material to the realm of the mind and spirit. We open ourselves for spiritual, mental, and intuitive perceptions and training.

Obelisks should be set up instead of laid down. Since this is only possible in the area of the foot centers or the head center, we set the obelisk into the "aura" next to the body in the area of the respective energy center, just as we do for other energy centers. We can also do this with large, heavy gemstones or with balls and eggs that roll away.

If the position of one or several of the stones changes after it has been laid on the person or even after Reiki has been given, we let this happen and do not put it back into its original position. In these cases, extremely fine stirrings within the body have led to the gemstone coming into an even better position for the momentary situation of the recipient.

When laying out and aligning the gemstones, we should be "completely into what we are doing" since we hold concentrated light energy in our hands with each gemstone. This very strongly activates the flow and acceptance of Reiki and its effect.

The Reiki Hand Positions

The basic positions for laying on the hands are taught with Reiki. These can be expanded through inner guidance in cases of acute pain and illness.

Our hands remain between two and five minutes in each position. It may happen that our hands become very hot or, in exceptional cases, ice-cold, or tingle when we give Reiki. It may happen that we feel the flooding of energy in our hands or that our body is also very warmly pervaded with it. We are therefore permitted to participate in the flow of Reiki and always receive a self-treatment in a very natural way when we give it to others. Even if we feel nothing of this at all, that does not mean that there is no flow of Reiki. It just means that we are not consciously perceiving it, for whatever reason. The experiences of many people who practice Reiki confirm this.

In addition, Reiki always orients itself towards the needs of the recipient and *not* what *we* want to give with it!

The hands should be placed without any pressure, slightly curved and thereby adapting to the form of the body. The fingers lie closed next to each other in a natural way in order to guarantee a concentrated flow of energy. Before and after giving Reiki, the hands should be cleansed under cold, running water. If we are wearing jewelry with which we don't want to be in conscious contact while we give Reiki, we should take it off. This also includes watches, and applies to the recipient of Reiki as well. Every piece of jewelry worn, by both the giver and the recipient, during the Reiki treatment comes into contact with the vibrations through Reiki. Jewelry also emanates and has an impact.

If a gemstone is to be placed on each energy center, the recipient should not wear a necklace, if at all possible. In most cases, the energy would then be too strongly activated in connection with the gemstones placed on the person. "Moderation" is also important in gemstone therapy. When too many gemstones are placed on a person for Reiki treatment, an overactivation can occur. The recipient may then "close up" or even show reactions ranging from tiredness to exhaustion.

The Reiki Partner Treatment

When we give a partner Reiki, this can be done in a sitting or prone position. A Reiki quick-treatment in a sitting position lasts about ten to twenty minutes, and a complete Reiki treatment while lying down can take from one to one-and-a-half hours. At the conclusion of the Reiki treatment in a prone position we can also do a chakra balance.

The Reiki Treatment in a Lying Position

This is the Reiki treatment with the most intensive effect. It lasts from one to one-and-a-half hours, includes the head, body, and back treatment and, if possible, should be given four times on four consecutive days at the beginning of a Reiki treatment series so that this daily flooding of all the energy systems triggers a major cleansing on all levels. It will set many things into motion, supporting us in a strong and powerful way. The body may eliminate toxins and deposited waste materials, and pain and chronic suffering may once again become acute and experience a loving treatment through Reiki. Such reactions cause us to once again confront the reasons of our suffering. Feelings are stimulated to more clearly express themselves. There are emotional reactions with the possibility of deepened insight for forgiving what has hurt us through painful experiences. Patterns of thinking and behaving, as well as concepts of self, become more conscious in their binding, constricting, blocking energy and are subject to the liberating light of Reiki. After this four-day initial treatment, there should be further Reiki treatments once or twice a week as an accompanying measure for situations such as an acute or chronic illness, a difficult crisis in life, a phase of life with examinations, or a big challenge.

When we give a partner a Reiki session, we should agree on an appropriate exchange of energy before we start. This can be a monetary payment or any other type of exchange. This is important since it protects the giver and the receiver from feelings of guilt, as well as false attitudes of expectation. It's not up to us to make a "promise of healing" since the power, for which we as a person initiated into Reiki serve as a channel, has a divine source. It bears within itself the universal knowledge of what the healing path of the recipient looks like, which experiences he will be permitted to make with his suffering in the future, for what purpose he still may need it, and when it will be relieved and resolved. We accompany and support this process of self-realization, self-perception, and healing with Reiki and the light powers of the gemstones. As mediators of the divine light, we thereby give the help and the power that the recipient now needs, that he himself has searched for, and that has led him to us.

We make sure that we give Reiki in a quiet, relaxed, and peaceful atmosphere. Soft meditation music and a fine fragrance support this. The partner who receives Reiki from us should feel himself accepted in love. When he lays down, we should be sure that he removes his watch and shoes, as well as any possible necklaces, and loosens tight-fitting clothing, belts, etc. Be sure he doesn't cross his legs in the prone position and that his arms rest next to his body. His eyes should be closed. We cover him with a wool blanket, if this is what he needs to be comfortable.

Even before we start giving Reiki, we cleanse our hands under cold, running water, free them of everything that they touched and did before, and separate ourselves from whatever we have been occupied with up to now. We wash our hands in "innocence." We are free of what happens, of what becomes activated through Reiki, and of what the recipient experiences. We are a pure channel that imparts Reiki.

If we include gemstones in this Reiki treatment and place them on energy centers, the light powers of these stones will be intensely activated and taken in by the recipient through the Reiki that flows during these one to one-and-a-half hours. We request inner guidance as to which gemstones would like to be placed on the person, select them intuitively, cleanse them, greet them with our Reiki hands, and lay them on the Reiki-recipient's body. The energy of the stones is best taken in above the energy centers, which is why these are the best places to put them. In the process, we make sure that they are facing in the optimal direction. When we do this, and also when we give Reiki, we should be on the left side of the partner since the body's left side is the receptive side and therefore particularly willing to accept Reiki.

At the beginning, we meditate briefly in order to become conscious of the fact that we are a Reiki channel, a mediator for the power of love and light from the divine source, and that concentrated light manifestations from this source, the positioned gemstones, accompany and support us.

In order to protect and activate, we smooth out the Reiki-partner's aura three times with one hand: we start on his left side where we are standing, move to the head, around the head, then down the right side of his body to his feet, around the back, and back up the left side of the body.

The Head Positions

We start the Reiki treatment with the Reiki head positions. We sit behind the head to do this.

1st Head Position

Without using any pressure, we lay our hands on the face, over the forehead, eyes, and cheeks. Reiki flows into the 6th energy center. On the physical level, it flows to the eyes, frontal and maxillary sinuses, nasal cavities, and sinuses of the nose. On the subtle level, the third eye becomes activated along with a perception of the correlations between spirit and matter; inner, intuitive vision; clairvoyance; the imagination, inspiration, and powers of inventiveness and fantasy; the soul's great powers of faith with its trust in divine guidance; as well as becoming conscious of and confronting rigid patterns of thought, excessive concepts of self, expectations and goals, dominance, ego, self-will, will, divine will, and helplessness and power.

2nd Head Position

Without any pressure, we place our hands at the side of the temples towards the eyes. Reiki has a calming and clarifying effect here that frees the thoughts and their burdening, binding, and narrowing powers. In addition, Reiki flows to the ears, sensitizes our consciousness for what we don't want to hear, and activates our inner listening - clairaudience or "second hearing."

3rd Head Position

We place our hands beneath the head; the fingertips touch the medulla oblongata (transition from neck to head). In doing this, Reiki activates and harmonizes the two halves of the brain in particular: on the right side, intuitive, associative, pictorial, and creative thought, and on the left side, the logical-

The Head Positions

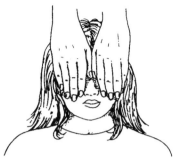

1st Head Position

2nd Head Position

3rd Head Position

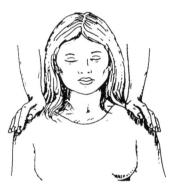

4th Head Position

5th Head Position

analytical, scientific, fact-oriented thinking so that both potentials are supported. Because the logical-analytical way of thinking in the left half of the brain is given biased support and training in our age, the right half of the brain is usually stunted and needs new impulses. In this specific position, the Reiki-recipient feels a great deal of protection and sense of security. He can thereby learn to entrust himself to the supportive, loving power of life and open up to new, creative, original experiences.

4th Head Position

We lay our hands gently on the edges of the shoulder. Reiki floods through the entire body down to the feet and evokes the experience expanding the physical consciousness and being freed from the weight of the material world.

5th Head Position

We gently form a triangle with our hands on the chest area. As a result, Reiki flows into the neck center and heart center. In the body, the vibrations of the thyroid gland, the metabolic activities, and respiratory tract of the bronchial tubes and lungs, as well as the breasts and heart, are filled with Reiki. On the subtle level, these are the vibrations of verbal expression, the inhibitions of speech, the suppressed emotions, the burdensome pressure, hurt feelings of love for ourself and other people who are particularly close to us, vibrations of the fears of separation and loss, the confrontations with giving and taking, self-pity, and unconditional love. This position is very special since it activates both the heart center and the neck center at the same time. The vibrations of both energy centers connect to form a special exchange of energy and mutually support each other. The liberated inhibitions and the greater freedom of self-expression permit a better flow of the heart's love; in turn, increased love in the heart allows us to communicate more lovingly.

The Body Positions

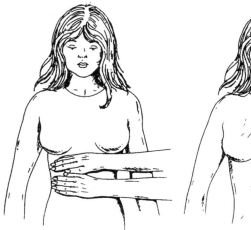

1st Body Position

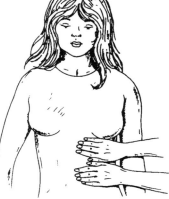

2nd Body Position

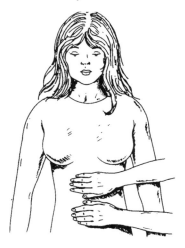

3rd Body Position

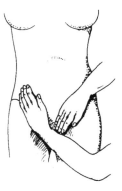

4th Body Position

The Body Positions

Now we move to the left side of the partner and maintain the body contact as much as possible with one hand while we do so.

1st Body Position

We lay both hands next to each other beneath the right breast. Here Reiki flows into the vibrational area of the 3rd energy center. Within the body, the liver and gallbladder are supported, as well as the stomach in part. In the subtle field of activity, this position supports confrontations with self-control and suppression, moderation and excessiveness (on all levels, the amount determines whether something is food, medicine, or poison), with will and self-will, and with power and helplessness. Correlations with the processes of the 6th energy center, the third eye, can clearly be seen here. But here these characteristics vibrate on a different level, namely in connection with the feeling of self-worth.

2nd Body Position

We lay our hands beneath the left breast. Reiki also flows to the areas of the 3rd energy center here: in the body, to the spleen, the pancreas, and partially also to the stomach. On the subtle level, the imbalances between openness and defensiveness, indifference and struggle, as well as the need for an exchange of tenderness, are touched by Reiki.

3rd Body Position

We lay our hands above and below the navel. The 3rd and 2nd energy centers are both activated at the same time here. Through this position, within the body Reiki flows into the digestive system, the stomach, as well as partially to the liver, gallbladder, pancreas and spleen, and the small and large intestines. On the subtle level, the transformation of the solid into the subtle is supported through the 3rd energy center. Furthermore, our "inner sun," our personal magnetism and aura, joy in life, courage and self-assurance are supported here, as well as the characteristics of permitting things to happen and letting go, movement and flexibility, and "being in flow" through the 2nd energy center. Tensions and imbalances, which lead to illnesses of the body after a certain time, are also affected in these regions. Examples of these through the 3rd energy center are envy, malevolence, mistrust, feelings of inferiority, excessive fear, as well as suppressed and swallowed emotions. Partnership problems, not only with the companion in life and the family, but also with a great variety of partnerships, the encounter with the other person, with things that are not so familiar and understandable for us, the blocking and restraint of vital feelings, all come through the 2nd energy center. The connection of these two energy centers through this Reiki position brings movement, flowing, and flexibility into our (blocked, obstructed) self-assurance and into our personal magnetism. On the other hand, the activated self-assurance within us helps us to accept what is new, unfamiliar, and suppressed with less fear so that we can let ourselves be increasingly carried by the living, vital stream of life.

4th Body Position

We lay the hands along the groin on the abdomen in the "V" position. Reiki flows particularly into our genital organs through the 1st energy center. It also activates the processes of elimination on the physical level. But the driving forces for coping with existence are also activated: initiative, motivations for living, sexual love and its enhancement, sublimation and transformation, partnership and family, reproduction, working life, career, the control of the drives, and liberation from dependencies.

If there are further, specific physical problems, we lay both hands on this place as well. For example, in the case of breast cancer, we place one hand on each breast. For painful knees, we put one hand on each knee, and for bronchial disorders we lay both hands next to each other on the sternum, with about ten to twenty minutes for each position.

The Back Positions

For the following back treatment, we remove the gemstones that are lying on the body and put them aside. We touch our partner and ask him to turn over and lay on his stomach; the arms should rest next to the body in this position.

With two exceptions, no gemstones are placed on the body for the back treatment. The first exception is that it may be necessary to lay a carnelian on the kidneys or within their area of influence during the entire Reiki back treatment when there are kidney problems. Secondly, for disorders of the bones, vertebras, discs, or spinal column, we put one green calcite on the coccyx (base of the spine). The carnelian supports the "flow," as well as all processes of decision-making and elimination. The green calcite brings a regenerating, loving power into what is broken, brittle, and rigid.

1st Back Position
We rest the hands next to each other on the back of the neck. Reiki flows to where the body and the head meet, which, on another level, also means it moves into the transitions from mind and matter.

The Back Positions

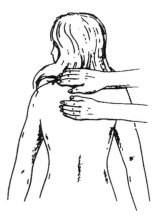

1st Back Position

2nd Back Position

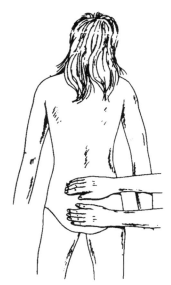

Coccyx (Base of the Spine)

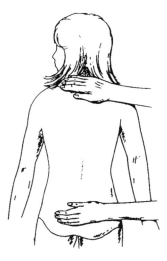

*Energy Flow through
the Entire Back*

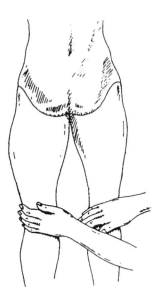

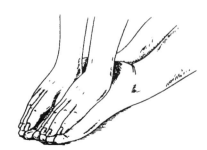

Fingertips on the Tips of the Toes

Hollows of the Knees

2nd Back Position

We place one hand on each shoulder. Then we slide the hands downwards so that one hand is on the left side next to the spine and one is on the right side next to the spine, without touching it directly, all the way down to its base. Within our back, we "hide" what we refuse to believe, what do don't want to look at, and don't want to show of ourselves. In the shoulder region, the burden that we have loaded onto ourselves, the experiences and decisions that weigh on us, and the feelings of guilt are touched. The upper part of the back is associated with fears and feelings of love from the heart, the ability to love, permitting relationships and contacts, and overcoming fears of loss. In the area of the kidneys, this relates to our centering, our focus, and the pelvic area shows our material level of existence and fears associated with it. On both sides along the spine there are nerve endings with which our center nervous system is activated.

We again put both hands next to each other above the **coccyx.** By doing this, we strengthen the Reiki energy above our "base."

Then we make contact with the starting point of the back treatment and put one hand on the nape of the neck so that one hand is located on the coccyx and the other on the neck. The beginning and end of the spinal column are activated, which produces a **flow of energy through the entire back** and an agreeable, tension-releasing harmonization.

If there are particular back problems, we can now place our hands next to each other directly on these areas and leave them there for ten to twenty minutes.

For holistic activation and grounding, it is very pleasant when the hands are laid on the **hollows of the knees** and/or soles of the feet: **fingertips on the tips of the toes.** This usually evokes a very reconciliatory feeling (conciliating a person with life on earth).

The head, body, and back treatment with Reiki should last about twenty minutes each, so that an entire Reiki session takes about an hour. If we leave the hands longer on certain individual areas of the body or additionally give Reiki to affected parts of the body, the Reiki session may extend to one-and-a-half hours. It also takes about this long if we do an additional chakra balance.

To end the session, we once again stroke the partner's aura three times and do an activating, restoring, and concluding *energy stroke* from the base of the spine to the head.

We give thanks for the gift of Reiki that we have experienced together, also thanking the gemstones and their powers of light. Then we cleanse the stones and our hands under cold, running water.

The Chakra Balance

We can give the chakra balance after the previously described 60-minute Reiki treatment. To do this, we ask the partner to turn over on his back and give the chakra balance without replacing the gemstones (about 10 minutes).

However, it is also possible to do the chakra balance after the head and body positions without giving a back treatment (about twenty minutes). In this case, the gemstones on the energy centers remain where they are since they provide a positive balance of the vibrations within the energy centers.

But we can also give the chakra balance without the previous Reiki treatment, putting gemstones either on all of the energy centers or specific ones that we have chosen with the help of intuitive guidance. In this case, we should take about half-an-hour for the chakra balance, which means approximately ten minutes for each main position.

The partner rests on his back. We place the cleansed gemstones on his body, move to his left, and stroke his aura three times.

1.) We very gently put our left hand on the 1st energy center and the right hand on the 6th energy center. The energy of both of these centers flows together in the process, achieve a unity, and support each other in an optimal exchange. At the same time, the activating, spontaneous energies of the 1st center, related to our life on earth and existential drives and needs, along with the divine consciousness of the soul's great power of faith that is known to move mountains and make possible the impossible, are united with the 6th chakra's reason, inner cosmic peace, and the powers of imagination and thought. A harmonization and stimulation between these two contrasting powers, matter and spirit, then becomes possible.

Chakra Balance

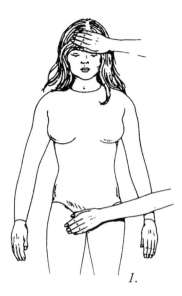

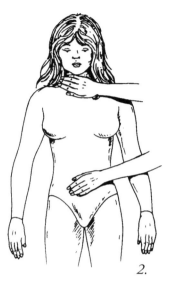

1.

2.

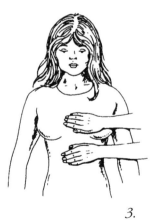

3.

2.) After about seven to ten minutes, we let our hands come closer to each other: we now place the left hand on the 2nd energy center and the right hand very lightly on the 5th energy center, only indirectly touching the throat. Here the powers of the living, vital flow, of allowing things to happen and letting go, merge with those of self-expression in language and the ability to communicate. We learn how to more fluently express ourselves and communicate through the language, thereby finding new possibilities for the encounter with others and with the unknown. Our partnerships and our communication with the surrounding world become more alive, more imaginative, and more joyful.

3.) Now our hands come even closer together. The left hand lies on the 3rd energy center and the right hand on the 4th energy center. The radiating sun of our "center" unites with the love of our heart. Our feeling of self-worth, and with it our personal magnetism, comes into a harmonious vibration through the love of the heart. The result of this is that the energies of excessive or fearfully reserved power and dominance come into a more proper relationship with other needs in life. The peaceful feeling of self-worth is a strong basis for the love of the heart showing itself with the entire personality to the outside world in a wonderful way. This personality no longer conceals itself behind false modesty, is no longer blocked because of hurt feelings or through humiliations felt to be unjust, but supported by the natural beauty of radiating love.

The love of our hearts finds its powerful path to the outside world, the sun in our center is freed from vanity, becoming intensified in its emanation and effect by love.

For the conclusion of this chakra balance, we once again stroke our partner's aura three times, give thanks, and put the gemstones aside in order to cleanse them later. We then bring the partner back into the here and now by touching his body.

The chakra balance is a wonderful way of balancing all the energies within us and has such a harmonizing and renewing effect because of how the various forces flow together. This process is supported when we lay one gemstone on each energy center. But we can just as well decide to just place a gemstone on the individual energy centers that require special activation.

If the gemstone that we have laid on an energy center isn't too large, we can place our hand directly over it. Reiki will then flow directly through the stone and its brilliant color rays flow into the energy center. But if the stone is very large, it is better to put your hand next to it.

The Reiki Quick-Treatment in a Sitting Position

For this Reiki treatment in a sitting position, it is quite easy to include a gemstone. This stone can be placed on the floor between the feet of the recipient or, even better, put in his hands as he holds them like an open bowl on his lap or thighs.

Before starting, we intuitively select the gemstone by preparing ourself inwardly, greeting it lovingly, cleansing it, and holding it in our Reiki hands so that its powers of light become activated. The gemstone's brilliant color ray rises and flows on its own to the place where our hands lie while we give Reiki.

If possible, we stand at the left side of our partner.

We lay our hands on the shoulders. Reiki flows into the pain areas of the shoulders: to experiences that weight us down, that we have "saddled ourselves" with, and as a result of which we have developed feelings of guilt.

We place one hand on the forehead, and the other hand on the back of the head. Reiki flows to the 6th energy center (forehead center, third eye).

We place one hand on the hollow of the neck, without directly touching the throat while doing so, and the other hand on the nape of the neck. Reiki flows into the 5th energy center (throat center).

We place one hand on the chest and heart area, and the other hand on the back at the same height. Reiki flows to the 4th energy center (heart center).

We place one hand above the navel and the other on the back at the same height. Reiki flows into the 3rd energy center (solar plexus center, "our center").

We place one hand below the navel, and the other hand on the back at the same height. Reiki flows into the 2nd energy center (sacral center, "flowing").

We place one hand on the abdomen, and the other hand on the coccyx (base of the spine). Reiki flows into the 1st energy center (base center).

In closing, we do an upwards "energy stroke" from the coccyx to the head center above the top of the head with one hand in order to stabilize the energy.

We give thanks for Reiki and the support of the gemstone, gently touch our partner so that he comes back into the "outside world." We later cleanse the stone and hold it in our Reiki hands.

This Reiki quick-treatment in the sitting position is a wonderful, energy-giving, stabilizing, restorative treatment and therefore suitable for "recharging." However, it also offers a very pleasant and effective method for giving someone a quick-treatment who would like to get to know Reiki. It should last from fifteen to thirty minutes.

The special thing about this treatment is that it simultaneously touches and activates the back and the front of the body. In the back we need support, security, stability, and protection for the front side of our body, with which we are very open and vulnerable. We take in all energies from the "front." Our energy centers open up to the front side of the

Reiki Self-Treatment

1.

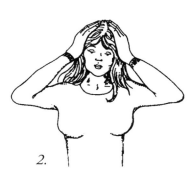

2.

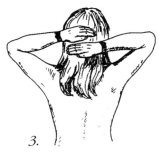

3.

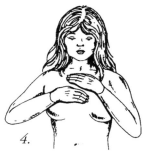

4.

5.

6.

body like flower cups, and we are in a constant state of energy exchange here. When both sides are supported with Reiki at the same time, the powers become strengthened and give us a feeling of pleasant stability.

Reiki Self-Treatment

We can carry out the Reiki self-treatment while sitting or lying down. In the sitting position, it is possible to place a gemstone with an energy that we want to include in the treatment between our feet on the floor after it has been prepared for this step. Its brilliant color ray rises during the self-treatment, and we particularly take it into the places where we lay our hands.

If we do the self-treatment in a lying position, we can place a gemstone on a specific or on all the energy centers and intensify the flow of Reiki in this manner. This happens on its own and especially at the spot where our hands are placed at the moment:

1.) First we lay both hands on our face, over the eyes (6th energy center)
2.) Then at the sides on our temples
3.) Then one above the other at the back of the head
4.) Then on the heart and chest (4th + 5th energy centers)
5.) Then one hand above the navel and one hand below it (3rd and 2nd energy centers)
6.) Then we form a "V" with both hands on the abdomen (1st energy center).

The effects of these Reiki positions on both our body and the subtle processes have already been described under "Reiki Treatment in a Lying Position."

Reiki Treatments with Seven Specially Selected Gemstones

Almost every type of gemstone is suited for use in a Reiki treatment. I have selected the most important gemstones from each color ray here and described their effectiveness. However, we should be aware that a great many more beneficial things occur than we can perceive or put into words.

Red color ray:
Garnet
Orange color ray:
Carnelian
Yellow color ray:
Amber, citrine, rutile quartz
Green color ray:
Chrysoprase
Pink color ray:
Rose quartz
Light-blue color ray:
Chalcedony, aquamarine
Dark-blue color ray:
Lapis lazuli
Violet color ray:
Amethyst
Radiates in clear light:
Quartz crystal

Seven Garnets

Joyful Development, Vitality, Initiative

If we put a garnet on each main energy center for the Reiki (self-)treatment, a strongly luminous, powerful red flows into all of the energy systems.

When Reiki is given, a great deal of light energy flows to the garnets and activates their brilliant red on the subtle level so that it increasingly ascends into the bright-red color stream of the universe. The beings of this color stream, connected with the ascending light energy of the garnet, "sense" this and feel themselves "called." This delights them since they have waited for such a moment since the time they allowed the garnet to grow within the earth. In this bright-red glowing and shining that rises to them from the earth, they can "descend" into the coarse vibrations of the material world. The garnet vibrations activated by Reiki let a red, luminous channel of light ascend in the red stream of light for every garnet placed on a person, so that the light beings of the garnet can come into the vibrations of the energy centers, and thereby into the energy processes of the Reiki recipient, through this ray of light. They let their powerfully luminous red be exuded into the garnet activated by their light energy through Reiki. This brings the required vitality, drive, spontaneity, and initiative typical of the garnet into all the energetic processes that are reached through our energy centers.

This is particularly helpful when a person feels himself to be very weak physically, after a longer period of illness, a substantial loss of blood, a lack of drive and motivation in life, and in phases of development, whether they be on a material, physical, existential, professional or personal level, or on another level.

The Garnet in the Individual Energy Centers

In the first energy center, the light-permeated red of the garnet strikes the dominating vibrations of the energy center and accordingly supports its main function: joyful development, the challenges of the material world, and the physical processes. For example, the garnet energy provides for healthy development of the blood and cells, a harmonization of the blood count, vital sexuality and drive, the development of a partnership and family, the satisfaction of needs relating to basic existence, for the development of a professional career, and an active, dynamic feeling for life.

In the second energy center, the powerful, life-giving, and impulsive bright-red vibration of the garnet intensifies the "flowing," the blood circulation and flow, motivates us to be spontaneous, creative, and take the initiative in confrontations with the "other," the partner, and in decision-making situations. It helps us act in a practical and an imaginative manner. The joy of success gives us momentum.

In the third energy center, the red garnet has a constructive effect on the renewal of the cells in the liver, gallbladder, stomach, spleen, and pancreas, as well as intensifying the decomposition and removal of waste materials. However, the garnet also strengthens our self-confidence, encourages us to be more dynamic and spontaneous in coming out of our shell, drives us on to having a greater belief in our own capability of doing and carrying out those things that are important to us. Courage combined with initiative helps us overcome blocks that hinder us.

In the fourth energy center, the heart center, the center of our love is strengthened with the flowing red garnet energy. On the physical level, particularly the heart muscle, and thereby the energy supply for all the tissue and circulation, are strongly vitalized. Our ability to love is set into joyful stimulation. Spontaneity supports us in opening up to more love and helps us became familiar with the blazing flame of our heart's love through the test of the fire power.

In the fifth energy center, the radiant garnet red comes into the throat center and activates the power of our verbal possibilities of expression. We practically bubble over in joy and find it easier to make new contacts and develop relationships.

In the sixth energy center, its red sparkle challenges our belief in outsell and develops the willpower to realize our plans and ideas and for satisfying our basic needs for existence. Initiative and power of belief allow high objectives to become reality.

In the seventh energy center, the red garnet vibration lets us meditate with joy and zeal. Within us, it intensifies the inspirations and ideas for the practical requirements of our everyday life. The joy in the abundance of possibilities, in both non-material and material affluence gives us the feeling of wealth on all levels.

When a lack of drive can be attributed to physical symptoms of deficiency, garnets cut into an oval form are of particular help, whether they are cut as cabochons or in facets. The cabochon is "softer," more gentle, and cautious in its drive. Each faceted, cut garnet is a focus and provides a further push for the activated aspects.

If the lack of drive tends to be of a psychological origin, if motivation is lacking, the emotions are intensely restrained, then the garnets cut in a teardrop-form, particularly those that are faceted and bright red, are helpful.

If there is a lack of impulse-giving, spontaneous ideas for new developments, the round forms in a cabochon or facet cut provide special support.

The round, cut garnet cabochon calms feelings that run high and thereby brings more composure into the world of thoughts.

The round garnet in the facet cut has an additional strongly concentrated effect in every activation energy.

For making the concepts of a new development concrete in an area of our life relating to basic existence, the square garnet in facets (usually in an octagonal cut) is the suitable helper since it not only evokes versatile joy and initiative for the development, but also manifests and translates it into physical reality.

On the one hand, we can select the same form for all the energy centers, but we can also attune each energy center in a differentiated manner and choose a special form that best corresponds to its respective needs.

The tumbled stone is appropriate for the general activation of the garnet energy on all levels and offers temporary help if you do not (yet) want to commit yourself to a specific stone. Later, the energy can be guided into a more distinct course through more specific forms. The bright-red vibrations and light beings that come to us through the garnet permeate us completely with this red. This is an intense activation that we should only select when a person is very exhausted, weak, lacking in drive, disinterested in life, or in a phase of recovery after an illness or operation.

Seven Carnelians

Flooding, Movement, "Being in the Flow"

For the Reiki (self-)treatment, we put a carnelian on each energy center. With Reiki, we let the stone's warm, orange light that flows into each energy center glow and merge into one strong, orange-colored energy stream. our entire energy system is flooded by it and the orange-colored ray in our life stream becomes very strong. The orange light vibrations ascend above each of the energy centers activated in this manner and into the world of the great cosmic color streams, "calling" the light beings of the carnelian into the material world, to their stone. They direct the orange-colored light of the carnelian that is permeated by Reiki into our energy system, with the result that this constantly flowing orange is capable of dissolving congestions, deposits, hardenings, and blocks. These are then carried away in this great flowing and streaming. On the one hand, this triggers an intensive, pulsating cleansing, as well as an energy charge that increases our feeling for life on the other hand.

The Carnelian in the Individual Energy Centers

In the first energy center, the carnelian brings move flexibility and elasticity, as well as a certain relief and sense of well-being into the more impulsive, aggressive energy potential that constantly drives us to safeguard our survival.

In the second energy center, the light energy of the carnelian flows into the main energy stream of this center, which vibrates in orange. The light beings of the carnelian support the "flowing" within us here. On the physical level, this has a special harmonizing influence on the blood circulation, the supply of blood, the blood pressure, and is very helpful for varicose veins. At the same time, the kidneys are flushed, cleansed, and relieved. The effect is very strong on the emotional level: in this center we experience the confrontation with the "other," the partner, with what experience as different and separate from ourselves, what we reject, admire, or need to master. The constant flowing, the permeating, pleasant warmth of the carnelian, permits us to approach our surrounding world in a more free, flexible, and creative way. It also helps relieve pent-up emotions and hardened attitudes. On the vibrational level of our thoughts, concepts, ideas, and ideals, the carnelian inundates us with its flowing and thereby moves the rigid thought patterns and frozen self-concepts into more generous paths, permitting us to be more willing to make decisions.

In the third energy center, the luminous orange of the carnelian brings us our "sun power," a flowing warm energy that supports more imagination in the radiation of our self-confidence, promoting relaxed behavior. We find the way back to our center from extreme modes of behavior.

In the fourth energy center, the carnelian energy strengths the work of our heart, sets into motion a sea of uncried tears from the soul's painful memories on the emotional level so that they can flow and make it possible for us to be relieved of and separated from oppressive, hurt feelings.

In the fifth energy center, the carnelian with its luminous orange enlivens our communication and our need to speak with others. Verbal inhibitions can more easily be resolved. When the respiratory system is afflicted, a pleasant, relaxing warmth flows through this area of the body with the carnelian.

In the sixth energy center, the brilliant orange-colored energy stream of the carnelian placed on the head imparts creative impulses to our thinking. The streams of thoughts enters into flowing vibrations that can more easily take up the ideas and imaginative inspirations, directing them on their way. High goals and ideals are freed from their one-sidedness and rigidity, and an animating momentum enters into our self-concepts and power of belief, driving off a certain boredom.

In the seventh energy center, the radiant orange carnelian helps us come into contact with our higher guidance and make decisions with divine intuition.

A Reiki carnelian treatment is particularly helpful when more momentum, flexibility, imagination, and lightness is needed.

For varicose veins, disorders of the blood circulation and blood pressure, as well as kidney problems, an oval carnelian

cabochon is particularly effective since this form lets the energy flow into the physical level.

If there are increased tensions in the area of partnership, the carnelian is more suitable in the form of a tumbled stone since we learn not to get stuck in "grating" situations through its constantly flowing energy. Instead, we develop abilities to deal with each other in a sensitive manner and be able to accept life despite all of the points of friction.

Seven Pieces of Amber

Success Treatment

The Reiki (self-)treatment with amber brings luminous honey-yellow into our life stream, making it possible for many sunlike beings to let us to share in their experience of joy and guide us to the people who help us achieve success.

The holistic flooding of our energy system with the joy of success dissolves on all levels the blocks, fears, and self-concepts that impede and prevent our success. This gives us the power and the endurance to reach a goal. A blissful feeling of being alive flows through us when we permit success to happen.

The Amber in the Individual Energy Centers

In the first energy center, success is particularly supported on the level of existence and the material world. We are guided to people who help us achieve things like professional, financial, and/or personal success. With their help, we find a house, an apartment, a partner, good business connections, suitable space for a practice ...

In the second energy center, the honey-yellow amber energy flows into the level of relationships and partnership. Here the sunlike beings dissolve the modes of behavior that time and again have disturbed (or destroyed) successful relationships or have prevented them from happening at all. They stimulate the creativity and imagination that lets us be successful in dealing with other human beings.

In the third energy center, the beings of the amber connect us with the dominating yellow vibrations of this center, with our "inner sun." This has strong effects on our self-confidence so that we can make changes within ourselves and permit great successes to occur. At the same time, we overcome our fears of encounters and challenges, feelings of inferiority, as well as excessive self-awareness, exaggerated ambition, and craving for admiration. Through our sunny personality, a spirited joy of being alive spreads to others and independently contributes to our presence being very much appreciated by everyone around us. Without desiring to do so, we stand at the center of attention and at the same time learn to develop and radiate a natural sense of self, generosity, and joy.

In the fourth energy center, the luminous honey-yellow of the amber connects with the love of our heart. Its angels evoke a great deal of warmheartedness, much joy and kindness, opening the door to success for us in this manner. We conquer the world in this vibration with "heart." The quality that lets us be successful in matters of the heart on the one hand, also supports all of our striving for success with sympathy and love on the other hand. We do not achieve success at the cost of others, but from a stance of joy and enthusiasm and love of life.

In the fifth energy center, the amber gives our voice a pleasant sound that can even be very tempting and seductive without seeming affected. This lets our communication be successful. On the physical level, the honey-yellow amber has healing effects on the congested respiratory system.

In the sixth energy center, the success-creating energy stream of the amber with its luminous yellow pervades our self-concepts that form mental structures and thought patterns. The sunny beings of the amber lay the foundation stone for a successful life expectancy here. We open up to a successful concept of life since we can imagine being successful.

In the seventh energy center, the amber supports success in meditation, in prayer, and in contemplation. Its light beings help us to be successful in searching our soul, in our encounter with the highest quality, though the development of steadfastness and endurance.

Pieces of amber are usually cut into fantasy forms, but can also be found as tumbled stones and in the cabochon cut. The size of the stone, its luminous yellow, and its inclusions decide how it has its effect even more than its outer form. Amber that tends towards a cognac-colored yellow evokes more of the earth-related power of success, while the lighter, sun-yellow supports success in the development and radiation of light energy on all levels. I primarily prefer to work with the luminous, lighter pieces of amber with inclusions that look like little suns. They promote our encounters with people who strengthen our sun-consciousness on our path in the light.

Even when we use tumbled stones, a vibration of success is activated on all levels. We can considerably increase it by laying a lovely, large piece of amber in the place of a tumbled stone on an energy center whose success emanation we would most like to intensify.

I recommend this success treatment with seven pieces of amber to all people who consciously or unconsciously long for success, yet are not joyfully successful. When a new chapter of life is at hand, when we start out on a new path, this treatment will blaze the trail for success. The amber with "sun inclusions" is a good-luck charm.

Seven Citrines

Wisdom, Translation
of Spiritual Perceptions

With the citrines, light-filled yellow comes into our life stream and our aura. Fine yellow rising into the light world is the signal for the light beings in the yellow color ray that they are needed on the earth. Bright with joy, they come to their manifestations, the citrines, whose light vibrations have become so strong through Reiki that its beings can come to us on the bright-yellow rays.

Very few citrines have grown in the ground as yellow citrines. Most of them are violet amethysts that have been give a heat treatment. The natural citrine and its light beings very strongly activate the wisdom of the soul that has already become conscious during past lives. It once again brings it intensely into consciousness and activates our spiritual life. It is a very fine and clear energy that touches a knowledge lying deep within us. We learn to once again bring it to the outside in simplicity and sublime stillness, letting our wisdom become more animated, visible, and livable.

The energy of citrines that were initially amethysts has a different effect. As amethysts, they were connected with the violet color ray, from whose light beings they were manifested on the earth. They come from the highest vibrational frequency, opening our consciousness above the head center for the highest intuition. As a result of the heating treatment, they became citrines and come into the yellow color ray with their vibrations. Their light beings also experience this "fire transformation" and come into the great yellow color ray, where they emanate the intrinsic wisdom of the sunlight to the earth. The connection of these two forces, intuitive wisdom and practicable wisdom, also occurs within nature in the amethyst, although this is quite rare. The ametrine is a stone, part amethyst and part citrine, that has united both powers within itself. It possesses and activates both: the connection with the high intuition and the wisdom of the soul that once again enters the conscious mind. Natural citrines and ametrines are very rare. This is why I describe the energetic effects of citrines that have been created by heating amethysts. Their special quality is the power of transformation from high to deep vibrations. The violet of high intuition, of turning to and opening up to the divine, still vibrates within them, yet they have come into a practicable energy of translation through the yellow color. The intuitive perception in violet is extensive, momentary, and not lastingly comprehensible. The integration and translation of this perception into daily life requires the yellow, the power of the sun that radiates brilliant light needed on the earth in order to express our light consciousness.

The citrine Reiki (self-)treatment accompanies each of us on our path with light. Within us, it supports the ability to translate intuitive perceptions of the divine into livable and teachable wisdom, letting it become perceptible with the help of the emanation and effectiveness of our self-confidence.

The Citrine in the Individual Energy Centers

In the first energy center, together with the citrine the brilliant and light-filled yellow pervades all of our fears, wishes, and needs related to existence. The nature of the citrine strengthens our self-confidence, which is sustained by highest intuition and divine wisdom. We are encouraged to include intuitively perceived truths in the mastering of our everyday lives and in the goals we set for ourselves. In the energy flow of divine wisdom, our fear of life (survival) disappear and our needs related to existence are transformed: the desire to live the divine in the earthly realm becomes increasingly strong and fulfills itself.

In the second energy center, the luminous yellow of the citrine flows into the confrontation with the "other," into the level of partnerships and relationships. Divine wisdom permeates our encounters, as well as what we reject and what we long for. We intuitively "know" how we should act towards others and we receive the power and courage to also translate these inspirations into action.

In the third energy center, the light beings of the citrine come into the main energy stream of this center, which is yellow. Here they greatly strengthen the sun power of divine self-fulfillment. Intuitively perceived wisdom becomes wisdom that can be experienced and brings our self-confidence into harmony with the divine will. The citrine's effect in this energy center is also strong on the physical level and the processes connected with it in our energy bodies. The digestive work of the stomach is particularly supported by the citrine's power of light, which turns from violet to yellow through a transformation, since a decisive conversion of the food received also takes place in the stomach. Not only what we have had to eat and drink is processed here, but also what we have done since there is a correlation with the way in which we feed our soul and our mind. The light beings of the citrine bring us more strongly and consciously into contact with the sun power, connected with the light in this food, and help us to absorb it in love and gratitude with the food we eat.

In this way, the earthly food becomes a divine meal with which our body, our soul, and our mind are nourished in loving consciousness.

In addition, the light beings of the citrine have a relieving influence on the liver, particularly on its detoxification work. Our own will merges with the wisdom of the divine will, no longer creating "poisoning" thoughts, emotions, and objectives.

The pancreas and the spleen are also influenced by the yellow light of the citrine. Our need for tenderness, which is connected with the insulin secretion of the pancreas, becomes stronger and desires that we live it out. The development of the body's defences occurs in harmony with divine wisdom and frees us from the need to be against something or someone as a matter of principle, of having to defend ourselves in a presumptuous or high-handed manner.

With the citrine's bright yellow glow, we are confronted with our shadow sides. At the same time, we are encouraged to let them become divine gifts through our wisdom.

In the fourth energy center, the light yellow of the citrine activates the wisdom of the heart. This frees us from exaggerated, falsely understood modesty and (self-) pity, releasing us from the cycle of suffering. We perceive the meaning of suffering and also that we only suffer as long as we do not "see" that we ourselves are the cause of this suffering. We always have the freedom to make the decision for either fear or love.

In the fifth energy center, the citrine animates our verbal expression with the divine wisdom that enters our consciousness. We become more courageous and able to communicate our light experiences through words and speak about what we have perceived. The inexhaustible knowledge of divine existence becomes more intense and understandable in our communication with others.

In the sixth energy center, the citrine with the luminous yellow touches our "divine eye" and intensifies our connection with the universal knowledge. Feelings of the omnipotence of the divine will and the powerlessness of the egocentric will come to "light," meaning that we become conscious of them. We are permitted to learn that power is a force of strength (of will) and to use it in the divine sense. As a result, we become more creative, devote ourselves to achieving the highest quality, become free of judgmental opinions and destructive self-concepts, and no longer need to control other people.

In the seventh energy center, the "heated" citrine finds its way back to the violet from which it was created. Experiences of enlightenment and light, as well as bright ideas, "illuminate" our consciousness and strengthen us in opening up to the wisdom of the universal spirit.

The activation of our energy is particularly effective if we place an uncut citrine tip on each of our energy centers with the tip pointing towards the head. A strong, shining yellow flame radiates through each energy center and merges in our energy bodies and life stream into a large, powerful yellow flame. This ignites an intensely glowing sun-power and radiant, completely enthusiastic self-confidence within us, burning away everything that is dark and frightening for us.

This Reiki treatment with uncut citrine tips brings a greater clarification and liberation from fearful patterns and the release of our sun-power, our light-filled emanation, with itself. This is particularly important if we are continually tormented by self-doubt, discouragement, depressions, act against our better knowledge, suppress ourselves and others, thereby binding and abusing power.

For complaints of the stomach, liver, and gallbladder, the pancreas and insulin secretion, and/or the spleen, and for increasing the body's defenses, the citrine is very helpful as an oval-cut cabochon on every energy center. Citrine cabochons in the round form on each energy center support us particularly when we suffer from a lack of self-confidence.

If we put a faceted, cut citrine on the energy centers, each facet with its light beings awakens a brilliant ray of sunshine within our being and radiates joy, life-giving warmth, and inspirational wisdom. All our shadow sides turn to the light, and we learn to transform ourselves and master our life with divine wisdom. This requires courage and the willingness to honestly open up to the fear of our great strength and power in order to then let go of it and be free to do what is wonderful.

At the same time, the oval form takes us beyond the physical level and brings light to the dark, meaning the afflicted, parts of the body. We perceive the meaning of this illness for ourselves. The teardrop shape lets the sunlight flow into the soul and gives us a sunny disposition. The round form "enlightens" our mind, gives us lucid thoughts and self-knowledge. The square form manifests the sun power that has awakened within us on the earthly, worldly level: we solve the problems of everyday life by translating the spiritual/mental perceptions into radiant self-confidence.

Seven Rutile Quartz Stones
Harmony, Golden Light, Blessing

The Reiki (self-)treatment with a rutile quartz on each energy center brings a great deal of golden, radiant pure light into our energy systems. It rises in golden, flowing light waves into the divine stream of blessings and to its light-bearers, who bring us a very special loving energy from our Creator. Just as the golden needles are manifest in the pure light of the crystal within their stone, they come to us as "messengers of the divine" with golden arrows of light.

The gold vibrations manifest in the "rutile needles" are as quick as an arrow and have a specific aim. They are surrounded by the pure light of the crystal, and this unique combination develops perfect divine harmony and beauty on all levels within us. The divine light in its pure beauty and beneficial power increases our light vibrations and makes us allies in the light on the earth, which sends out harmony and blessing through the "arrows of light."

In the physical processes, the strong harmony and beneficial/loving connection with our Creator evokes the relief from pain and brings healing. In the vibrations of the soul, extreme mood swings and inner conflict are resolved. On the intellectual level, the energies of thoughts and mental structures are guided in a divine direction by the luminous arrows of light.

The Rutile Quartz in the Individual Energy Centers

In the first energy center, the pure, radiant golden light of the rutile quartz connects us, through its light-bearers, with the basic needs of our soul to live our life on earth in honor of the Creator and for the blessing of the Creation, of which we are a part. Respecting and observing the divine beauty, joy, and radiance in each encounter and lively, loving solidarity with all of Creation makes our life on earth rich in joy, harmony, and blessing, free from worries and hardships related to existence here. Each encounter, each deed becomes an experience and an exchange of divine love in its perfected beauty.

In the second energy center, the golden, luminous light flows through the rutile quartz and its light-bearers into our conflicting emotions and our inner struggles in living with others. In this flow of energy, we learn to particularly appreciate the others in their special characteristics and create a new quality within partnership relationships: supportive, imaginative, pleasantly relaxed, and engaging when we are together, emphasizing the unique beauty of each individual.

In the third energy center, the rutile quartz permeates the main energy stream of this center, which vibrates in yellow. Its bright, gold-flooded light increases the vibration and radiation of our inner sun so that our self-confidence strongly expresses itself as inner joy, beauty, harmony, and generosity.

Here the golden arrows of light in the rutile quartz help us to especially develop divine qualities in how we approach our inner modes of acting and reacting, assuming responsibility for the resulting effects and developing mastery with our self. We liberate ourselves from unconsciousness, as well as from emotions and ways of behaving that make us dependent on drives and addictions. True (self-) control occurs on the basis of loving life and liveliness.

In the fourth energy center, many experiences that burden the heart are resolved on their own with the rutile quartz since its golden arrows of light strike our hurt feelings and bring them the message of the divine love that understands everything. The pain of our heart that bears the soul's deep anguish at not being loved enough, must no longer defend itself against the strong power of love. We can open ourselves more in our heart energy and permit love to happen. The fear of once again being injured in this openness is carried away by the golden arrows of light.

With the pure, gold-saturated light, the gates open to the innermost place of our temple of light, if this is meant to be. Here holy healing, blessing, consecration, and initiation into the holy mystery of the divine await us. We are permitted to return to our divine origin, to the Great Mother, to the Heavenly Father. We are allowed to experience our divine rebirth and consciously receive our divine gifts for this life. The omnipotence of love unfolds in our human and divine personality, becoming a blessing for human beings and the earth with all its creatures.

In the fifth energy center, the light beings of the rutile quartz radiate harmony and beauty into our verbal expression. The words that we speak or write are permeated with divine spirit and spur us and others onwards. However, the golden arrows of light also bring harmonizing, healing energy to the bronchial tubes, the lungs, the respiratory tract, and quite specifically to the thyroid gland. In the case of functional disorders of the thyroid gland, they have a balancing effect: we come away from extreme mood swings and find our way to a pleasant state of liveliness. This strengthens our sense of well-being and gives us a harmonious feeling for life.

In the sixth energy center, the beings of the rutile quartz activate the golden light in our "divine eye" with their arrows of light, giving our will an increased orientation and purposefulness for the fulfillment of the divine will. Our concepts and thoughts, ideas and ideals turn to the highest quality. Divine beauty reveals itself in everything, and we perceive the harmony of the creation.

In the seventh energy center, the rutile quartz's brilliant golden arrows of light lead us to the highest mystical experiences of divine light. Our resistance, excuses, fears, and blocks melt away in the shining golden stream of light. We come into contact with the eternally loving divine consciousness on an inconceivably high level.

For physical pain and illnesses, a rutile quartz in the form of an oval cabochon on each energy center is particularly helpful since its radiant golden arrows of light most rapidly flood the body cells that vibrate in imbalance with the harmony of our Creator's love for us.

When people tend towards inner conflict in their emotional and mental worlds, have no idea what they want, use up their energy in considering and reconsidering, we should place a rutile quartz in the teardrop shape on each energy center. The form of the teardrop unites the opposites and expresses them in perfect beauty: the rounded, receptive portion and the directed tip.

A round rutile-quartz cabochon on each energy center brings harmony into the world of the mind. If we think too much, find no peace because of constantly circling thoughts, always think the worst, the light-bearers of the rutile quartz direct strong light thoughts to us in this rounded form through their radiant golden arrows of light.

The rutile-quartz energy flows into completely different dimensions when we put a rutile-quartz pyramid on each energy center. In the process, the deciphering of the holy mystery is activated, and we are permitted to immerse ourselves in the brilliant golden light.

86

If we put a rutile-quartz egg on each energy center, new things are permitted to happen, the highest creative power is supported and activates us through every arrow of light.

With a rutile-quartz ball on each energy center, we come into the vibrations of holy healing. Our deepest injuries are touched by the highest divine love so that we give up our own willfulness and self-pity and can open up to the blessing of healing. We recognize on the deepest level that we no longer need the pain of injury in order to remain in contact with our Creator. We find an infinitely blissful connection in the light.

Seven Chrysoprases
"Dying and Developing," Regeneration

With chrysoprases on each energy center, a gently shimmering apple-green stream of light flows into our energy system, into our stream of life. Its light-saturated green rises up into the great cosmic green stream of light and calls its beings to earth. This gentle green, coming to us through the chrysoprases and their light beings that shimmer in green, brings us the power of regeneration and renewal. We can develop a freer approach to dying and developing, to giving and taking. Our fears of what is new, of the unknown, of great changes, and of total devotion to life are an obstacle to us in finding a natural exchange of energy. With their luminous green, the light beings of the chrysoprase clear the path for us for natural healing and take away the fear of dying and of completely devoting ourselves since they connect us with our light-birth in the spiritual world. We experience not only the one side, death on the level of the material world, but also the other side—the birth of our soul on the level of the spirit.

Our true self is immortal and only its vibrational state changes, travels to other planes, and uses various bodies.

We learn to let go of our fears and open up to power, joy, and spontaneity in many areas of our life. This makes the chrysoprase Reiki (self-)treatment into a fountain of youth that constantly renews the liveliness, the "yes" to vital life, time and again letting us radiate as fresh as a dewdrop, in gentle beauty.

The Chrysoprase in the Individual Energy Centers

In the first energy center, the gentle green of the chrysoprase flows into our fears related to existence and death. On the physical level, this has the effect of more easily dissolving dead cells, healing sick cells, and permitting new and healthy cells to grow more quickly and in a greater number. In the mastering of our everyday life, we feel ourselves free of fears, even if we haven't succeeded in doing everything that we planned to do. We are more open for new impulses and the constantly recovering and renewing vitality of our body.

In the second energy center, the fine, gently shimmering green of the chrysoprase connects with our fears regarding relationships, with our fears of losing the people we love, with our fears of opening up to people who seem strange and different to us. The radiant green of the light beings of the chrysoprase reveals new areas of experience and new possibilities for approaching the "other," bringing renewal into our relationships and letting them become an elixir of life for us and others.

In the third energy center, the lustrous green energy stream of the chrysoprase and its light beings promotes a self-assurance that continually renews itself. We become free of having to prove to ourselves and our surrounding world that we are stronger, better, more powerful, bigger, etc. than other people. We learn to immerse in the power of giving and taking without wanting to "dish out" and having to "put up" with things. Our natural authority and beauty develops and radiates.

In the fourth energy center, there is a special connecting to the chrysoprase with one of the two main streams of energy, which vibrate in green and pink. Its green animates the green light stream of our heart center with very gentle energy, and its light beings touch our ability to love. We can let go of the pain that has remained from injuries to this love in our hearts, particularly the anguish in connection with the loss of a beloved person, pain of separation, and the resulting fears of separation. The regenerating power of the chrysoprase frees us from clinging to such experiences and lets us find liberation in the love of the heart.

In the fifth energy center, the chrysoprase relieves irritations of the respiratory system and respiratory organs with its gentle green. On another level, it supports our verbal expression with the love of the heart: our words and the sound of our voice have a natural and loving effect. We can dissolve speaking inhibitions and difficulties of verbal expression in the energy of "dying and developing." Then we can also communicate what once caused us fear, and we will be rewarded with successful experiences.

In the sixth energy center, the chrysoprase animates the visual faculty of our eyes with the energy of regeneration on the basis of its green stream of light and its light beings. Our third eye, the "divine eye," is also activated so that we can permit the "death" of our notions, thoughts, self-concepts, ideas, and ideals that do not promote our further spiritual development and take in new impulses and inspirations. This simultaneously has a refreshing effect on our mental world, which often tires us with bogged-down or constantly circling thoughts.

In the seventh energy center, the chrysoprase energy intensifies our confrontation with "all" and "nothing." We increasingly perceive that everything we can imagine and that we long for is already there. And yet, nothing comes into our earthly life that wasn't meant to be and that isn't animated with love. It is only love that makes it possible for us to let go, forming and experiencing something new at the same time. This is the secret of regeneration.

When we need renewing power in a very general respect, which helps us let go of the old on all levels and make room for something new, a Reiki (self-)treatment with chrysoprase tumbled stones offers the most suitable support. Its gentle green flows through our energy system with the power of nature.

For physical disorders, after operations, for disrupted and afflicted cell growth, for destroyed tissue, etc., the chrysoprase cabochon in an oval form lends special support to regeneration on each energy center. In the natural signs of fatigue or the body's aging process, this is also a refreshing vitalization of our physical powers.

If we are afraid of new modes of behavior, experiences, and life situations, the chrysoprase cut in the teardrop shape gives us more trust in the power of love. This means that fear can lose its power and be transformed into natural liveliness and beauty. The fear of dying, of devotion and selflessness, as well as the fear of death, can also be liberated and lead us to inner peace.

When we want to quite consciously confront "dying and development," what is transitory and eternal, as well as find new views of the world. self-concepts, and patterns of action, we should place a round chrysoprase cabochon on each energy center. The spirit perceives its immortality, our mental world expands and no longer torments us with senseless questions about the meaning of suffering and life. Coming and going is "seen" in the great cosmic context.

The Reiki (self-)treatment with a chrysoprase on each energy center is appropriate when we long for renewal and regeneration, as well as when we are confronted with death, no matter on which level, and would like to find our way to a natural attitude and liberated approach to giving and taking on all levels.

Seven Rose-Quartz Stones
Gentleness, Unconditional Love, Blossoming

When we place a rose quartz on each energy center for the Reiki (self-)treatment, an intensified pink-colored light is radiated. It then rises up into the cosmic pink luminous color stream and brings the light beings of the rose quartz such a loving greeting of light from the earth that they feel themselves attracted and come to us in their softly radiant pink, intensely animating the pink in our life stream and energy system, filling us with unconditional love. With this very fine, shimmering rose-quartz energy, the great power of gentleness is promoted within us, which melts away every form of resistance, imbalance, and imperfection with infinite divine wisdom, love, and kindness and allows what is beautiful, fine, and delightful to blossom within us like a rose. This develops our spirituality out of the love of our hearts with a sympathy for all of Creation.

This beauty and wisdom of the heart that blossom in the gently radiant pink of the rose quartz and its light beings brings us into intimate contact with the essence of the love that is more than personal, unconditional, and divine. It activates the pink flame of understanding, forgiving, melting away, and blossoming so strongly within us that our emotional body is purified of vibrations that are oppressive and egoistic. In our many lives on the earth, we are reunited time and again with the life streams that we do not harmonize with. This happens until we have dissolved, released, and redeemed every loveless, rejecting, oppressive, destructive feeling with unconditional, loving understanding and forgiveness, as well as sympathy.

The essence of love is what the rose quartz has in common with Reiki. The combination of both forces strengthens within us the burning desire to be in harmony with all living creatures and the divine within us, as well as the desire to merge into everything, living and loving in the blossomed wisdom of our hearts in perfect beauty.

The Rose Quartz in the Individual Energy Centers

In the first energy center, the rose quartz increases our quality of life with its gentleness and enriches the active, vigorous energy of this center, which is directed towards securing what we need to exist and affluence, with the striving for spiritual development in our life. The divine meaning of our existence, unconditional love, reveals itself and pervades and motivates us more and more in order to let the essence of love become effective in our life and therefore on the earth with all the powers available to us.

In the second energy center, the rose-quartz energy flows into the confrontation with the "other." In the light of the pink flame of love, our partnerships and relationships are released from oppressive, obstructive vibrations and, if it is meant to be, directed into fructifyingly creative relationships that create beauty. This produces support of each other and mutual spiritual growth.

In the third energy center, the gentle pink-colored shimmer of the rose quartz and its light beings help us to be able to "melt." As a result, humbleness and strength develop at the same time in our self-confidence, we find our way to a harmony despite crass mood swings and extreme experiences, and the great power of universal love is expressed in our very personal, individual way. Beauty from the blossoming of the soul comes out into our surrounding world and gives our appearance and our personal magnetism a sense of something splendid and fine.

In the fourth energy center, the pink of the rose quartz supports the pink-colored main energy stream of this center, which flows next to the other main energy stream of green. Here the light beings of the rose quartz very intensely activate the pink flame of divine love, the pure love of the heart. It is the sublime and unconditional love that understands and forgives everything. It is free of all human expectations, dependencies, and burdens. To the degree in which we can open up to this love and develop it in our life on earth, growth will occur in the wisdom of our heart, in addition to our spirituality. It is the beauty that comes from within and touches every person in his heart and in his soul on its own.

In the fifth energy center, the rose quartz has effects on our use of language and on our verbal manner of expression. Our communication becomes increasingly free of irate, accusing, derogatory, and envious ... undertones. The love of our heart speaks through our words. At the same time, this frees us of the oppressive pressure that lies on our heart and chest since this way of communicating "builds us up" and elevates both our soul's vibration and our mood.

In the sixth energy center, the rose-quartz energy flows with its gentleness into the "divine eye," opens us up to the perception of beauty, releases us from high-handed self-concepts, and brings us closer to our true divine existence. The pink flame of unconditional love melts away our tendency to judge and condemn. This produces common sense on the basis of the wisdom within us and lets us be a role model for many people without our desiring this or consciously emphasizing it.

In the seventh energy center, the rose quartz permits the love and beauty of the light world to be revealed to us through the highest perception. This is emotional nourishment for our innermost longing for unification with the divine.

The rose-quartz Reiki (self-)treatment is particularly helpful when we are dissatisfied with ourselves and the world, when we fight with a strong resistance within ourselves and our environment and when we are (or have become) loveless. It helps when we become more familiar with the great power of gentleness and want to express all that is fine and loving.

If we want to set into vibration the gentle qualities within us and thereby melt away resistances, we should place rose-quartz tumbled stones on our energy centers. When we use certain forms, the energy of the rose quartz flows into special areas of our being.

A rose quartz with a cabochon cut in oval form on each energy center teaches us a great deal of gentleness in dealing with our body, with its needs and pains. We find a loving approach to the body's organs and functions. This allows a delightful, pleasant, and fine harmony to flow through our body, giving it healing and beauty. We become more aware of the fine, subtle processes and correlations of our body, and we learn to love and respect it for the wonder that it is.

Teardrop-shaped, cut rose-quartz cabochons melt away our soul's pain and sensitize us to its beauty that desires to blossom. This is particularly helpful when we occupy ourselves with painful experiences and feelings from the past time and again, unable to separate from them.

The round rose-quartz cabochon on each energy center helps us to imbue our mental world with the universal love found in the wisdom of the heart and let go of oppressive thoughts. Our consciousness opens up to the essence of love, which wants to awaken what is fine, noble, beautiful, and gentle within us.

Even more loving consciousness develops in our life when we lay a rose-quartz pyramid onto each of the energy centers.

When we point the pyramid to the head with one corner (cf. pg. 41), increasingly more unconditional love flows into our earthly existence from the high levels, concentrating and structuring us in loving alignment. When the base of the pyramids that have been positioned points to the head, we send our spiritual love "upwards" and make this power available to the cosmos. A radiant pink pyramid of love unfolds above us, with loving healing energy for the earth and the people around us.

If we put a rose-quartz egg on each energy center, our creative powers are more strongly connected with the flowering of our spirituality so that the experience of selfless love in our life is embodied and we are permitted to support others in experiencing healing through unconditional love. This intensifies such things within us like the need to not only give outsell Reiki, but also give it to others, and helps us find an appropriate "framework" within which to do this.

A rose-quartz ball on each energy center intensifies and fulfills our need for unity with God in the pink flame, the need for the gentleness and the beauty of unconditional love. Our consciousness of effective universal love becomes perfected. With this power, all resistance melts away and our trust in boundless love is strengthened.

Seven Chalcedonies
Verbal Communication, "Speaker's Stone"

The chalcedony is a light-blue stone, often traversed by white wave lines. When we put it on each energy center for a Reiki (self-)treatment, light-blue waves with white-caps flood through our life stream and energy system. Its pale-blue color, traversed with white, rises up into the great cosmic light-blue color ray and calls its light beings to earth. They support us through the chalcedony in our verbal expression and help us to better communicate our thoughts and feelings and everything that "moves" us, thereby intoning that we are "heard." We learn to communicate appropriately with the chalcedony so that this is accepted and can be understood by others, powerfully but without "exploding" or "swallowing" what we have to say.

The Chalcedony in the Individual Energy Centers

In the first energy center, the chalcedony with its light beings helps us be better able to speak about our feelings and fears, desires, needs, longings, plans, and goals related to matters of existence. On another level, the vibrations of light-blue traversed with white have the effect of letting us come into fluent communication when we are angry, aggressive, or excessively fearful and blocked.

In the second energy center, the chalcedony evokes creativity and imagination in the communication with our partners in conversation. We can impart what moves us, what we expect from the other person, which fears inhibit us, which preferences and suggestions we have to contribute, etc. In this energy center, the chalcedony helps us to come into a stronger state of flux, become more flexible, nimble, agile, and willing to communicate through our more fluent verbal expression.

In the third energy center, the chalcedony with its blue-white wave-shaped vibrations supports us in expressing through the language what we can't "stomach." It encourages us to not get rid of what we have "swallowed" through stomach irritations, vomiting, or diarrhea, but instead communicate what has "hit home" with us and how it has done so. We learn to communicate from our center, with an agreeable self-assurance and a pleasant-sounding voice.

In the fourth energy center, the language of our heart is intensified. We can better convey in words the feelings of our heart, our love, as well as our innermost injuries, humiliations, and rejections. As a result of this, we can stop taking offence and withdrawing in order to punish ourselves and others. The beautiful and loving aspects of our being can then be more strongly expressed.

In the fifth energy center, the pale blue of the chalcedony with its white waves flows into the main energy stream, which is light-blue. It brings movement into this center, not in a stormy or vehement manner, but gentle like the pale-blue-and-white waves of the stone. Here it very strongly supports the willingness and ability to communicate and have an exchange of ideas through the language. Verbal expression becomes powerful and fluent. We learn to "play" with the language, be creative, build up contacts, and, if we so desire, communicate with "the entire world." In this energy center, which is also called the communication center, the chalcedony stimulates our flow of speech and self-expression through the language, encourages us to overcome inhibitions and gives us a sensitive feeling for the "right" word at the proper time.

In the sixth energy center, the chalcedony supports inner communication with the spiritual world and helps us quite naturally "speak" with the spiritual guides, helpers, angels, ascended masters, and light-allies. This opens us up to new possibilities of being connected and to an energy exchange with the light beings.

In the seventh energy center, the chalcedony brings movement into our communication with the "highest" and makes it possible for us to more reliably listen to our inner voice and respect the intuitions from the light world. Our meditations and prayers become true communication with God.

We give the chalcedony-Reiki (self-)treatment when we would like to express ourselves more fluently and better in language, whether it be oral or written, or when a situation especially requires this, such as a lecture, difficult negotiations, an important discussion, writing an examination, a book, a report, or when there are verbal inhibitions.

It is best to use tumbled stones when we would like to generally communicate in a more fluent and easy manner.

Chalcedonies in a cabochon cut support our abilities to communicate on various levels. If we place a chalcedony in oval form on each energy center for the Reiki treatment, verbal inhibitions, as well as suppressed, swallowed communications, can more easily be dissolved. A round cabochon on each energy center tends to round off our use of the language by giving it the "finishing touch" and therefore also has a very beneficial influence on our creative communication. If we want to be creative and inventive, expressing something new, a chalcedony egg on each energy center is helpful.

A chalcedony ball on each energy center supports communication that is worldwide and eloquent.

Seven Aquamarines

Balsam for the Soul, Holy Healing

When we put an aquamarine on each energy center for the Reiki (self-)treatment, a radiant blue light channel develops, which completely permeates us with the bright blue and rises up into the world of light, to the light beings of the light-blue ray in the universe. The light beings of the aquamarine come in this light channel with their bright blue into our life stream, into our energy system, and bring along balsam for our soul. It is the loving, healing comfort from our Creator for our feelings of loneliness, of abandonment, of separation, of being cut off, of injustice, and for the wounds of our soul. The depth of the ocean and the endless expanse of the sun-filled heavens stream into us with the aquamarine, letting us also be pleasantly expansive and free, and yet still protected. Within our soul, the luminous blue of the aquamarine also touches the longing to be a healing channel for the divine healing energy and for holy healing. An aquamarine frequently leads us, without being aware of it, to Reiki and supports us greatly in our state of being a Reiki channel.

When the luminous blue of the aquamarine in connection with Reiki spreads through our energy centers in all areas of our being, holy healing becomes effective on a number of levels. It may be that we very much need this energy in order to heal our hurt feelings and "bathe" ourselves in the light blue. When we give the aquamarine Reiki (self-)treatment on a more frequent basis, it may be that the qualities of the soul within us may be activated for receiving and passing on the divine healing power. In addition, very special gifts and abilities can develop in the state of being a healing channel. These are intensified by the divine healing power that flows through us since our soul potential has become conscious and vibrates along with it.

The Aquamarine in the Individual Energy Centers

In the first energy center, the aquamarine brings more expansiveness and freedom into our needs and goals related to daily existence with its luminous blue. It helps us to become more free of the self-imposed constraints in everyday life. We come into contact with our infinite possibilities of tackling problems, demands, and challenges, becoming more open for a constructive way of working with others, as well as with our spiritual guides and companions in the world of light. We are permitted to experience into the depths of our soul that we are not alone.

In the second energy center, the bright blue of the aquamarine intensifies the "flowing" and the confrontation with our surrounding world in its own way. It stimulates us to communicate from soul to soul. And it stimulates us to enter into relationships and partnerships that challenge us and let us become whole and healed.

In the third energy center, the energy of the aquamarine with its light helpers flows like balsam to our injured feelings of self-worth. It helps us find our way out of constricting feelings and ways of thinking, developing more expansiveness, a good grasp of things, and a comprehensive consciousness. We learn to be alternate between being at the center and in the background of whatever is happening. Then we radiate a healing repose.

In the fourth energy center, the aquamarine leads us to a healing perception: we should generously give what we have been longing for ourselves. Our heart center is filled with love from an infinitely inexhaustible divine source. Within this love, we are always willing to give love, understanding, affection, appreciation, and gratitude in abundance instead of demanding or expecting it from others.

In the fifth energy center, the bright blue of this aquamarine flows into the main energy stream of this center. Here it supports the verbal communication with our fellow human beings just as strongly as it does the communication with our friends in the spiritual world.

Our light friends can then find us as light channels for the imparting of healing messages and healing energies. As a result of the channeled energy, the recipient of these messages clearly senses that they come through us, but not from us. Holy healing touches us in our deepest, innermost place, in both giving and receiving, brings us relief from the pressure and constraint that we have imposed upon ourselves and puts an end to oppressive communications.

Verbal inhibitions are often based on excessive demands. Too much pressure, expectations that are too high, and demands weigh upon us. The luminous blue of the aquamarine gives us the necessary expansiveness here in order to allow ourselves the free space we need. It helps us communicate without fear.

In the sixth energy center, the "divine eye" receives the light energy of the aquamarine. This means that our vision is expanded, freeing itself from narrowmindedness, so that the healing consciousness becomes stronger. We can then better recognize the correlations between spirit and matter and perceive the effects of our thoughts, feelings, and actions. Our oppressive thoughts transform themselves into healing thoughts. They strengthen us in our reflections on how we can help others. Our insight leads to circumspection: we will better understand ourselves and others.

In the seventh energy center, the endless expanse and freedom in the bright blue of the aquamarine brings us closer to deciphering our holy mystery. Within each of us there is a divine plan laid out in the stream of life, which is to be "experienced" and through which wisdom is revealed in its liveliness and fulfilled on earth. With the aquamarine energy, the vibrations of the head center are liberated as much as possible from confining, limiting expectations so that healing can occur, even in the ways and in places where we do not expect it. In this dimension, our willingness and ability to permit healing without self-limitation is supported.

When we feel ourselves oppressed by worries, hardships, obligations, and constraints—and long for more repose, expansiveness, and freedom—we should do the Reiki (self-)treatment with an aquamarine tumbled stone on each energy center.

The aquamarines that have been cut as cabochons bring greater balsam for the soul. We take the oval forms if we suffer from physical pain caused by stress. Teardrop shapes are helpful when we are suffering from loneliness, need more comfort and sympathy, and would like to free ourselves from confin-

ing modes of behavior and relationships. We decide on the round shape if we would like to consciously develop healing thoughts. In the square form, our existence as a light channel is more strongly manifested and becomes a solid component of our everyday life.

While the aquamarines cut as cabochons activate and channel a wonderful, gentle healing power, the aquamarines cut in facets are like radiant stars on each energy center and in our life stream. They illuminate our gifts of holy healing within our healing channel and give us highlights in life.

If we choose the round form in a facet cut, we will become increasingly familiar with our healing gifts. In the faceted teardrop shape, the soul's need to be a healing channel is awakened. With the oval form, we experience the flowing of divine healing power through our physical perceptions. The square shape gives us much support from the spiritual world to let a center of spiritual healing be created here on earth.

Seven Lapis Lazuli

Power of Faith, Divine Guidance, Cosmic Peace

The Reiki (self-)treatment with a lapis lazuli on each energy center floods us with a deep-blue stream of light: a stream of light that has sparkles of gold running through it when there are pyrite inclusions in the lapis lazuli. This deep blue bears something holy within itself and, with its shimmering gold rays, reminds us of the starry heavens at night. When this stream of light, intensified by Reiki, floods through our life stream, this deep blue with golden "twinkling stars" rises into the great cosmic dark-blue ray and calls the high spiritual beings to earth here. They come from the homeland of our soul, to which we are permitted to return every night while we sleep, and bring divine wisdom into our consciousness. Cosmic peace touches our soul's power of faith, with which we can "move mountains." The star powers from our light family come to us through the sparkling golden pyrite inclusions. These are high spiritual helpers and guides in the light, which have taken on the task of bringing our willfulness into harmony with the divine will and sensitizing us for divine guidance through the activation of the high intuition. When we vibrate in this energy, we have more and more insight into the homeland of our soul and greater participation in it. We feel ourselves woven into the universal processes and develop responsibility for our perceptions, realizations, and objectives.

The Lapis Lazuli in the Individual Energy Centers

In the first energy center, the dark-blue of the lapis lazuli with golden pyrite sparkles evokes faith and trust in the abilities and power within us, with which we master the challenges related to existing in our earthly life in the great energy stream of divine wisdom and guidance.

In the second energy center, it gives us great trust in the encounter with others and with our environment, helping us recognize the meaning of being (brought) together. We discover what we can do for each other, perhaps even find mutual tasks, and learn how we can provide support and enrichment for others without losing ourselves.

In the third energy center, the lapis lazuli challenges us to be genuine and true, as well as finding harmony and peace within ourselves. The strengthened power of faith helps us do this, radiating with complete conviction the wisdom that desires to be revealed and lived out. Our personality emanates wisdom from the divine source.

In the fourth energy center, the divine will connects with the love of our hearts through the lapis lazuli and strengthens within us the trust in accepting and living the wisdom of this love. The soul's great power of faith finds access to the love of our heart and frees us from the primeval fear of not being loved enough. Because of this fear, we enter into many compromises, suffer, let ourselves be injured, and hurt others. With the growing love of the heart, we find the way to our true self and must no longer fear being "worthless." We are no longer dependent on the esteem of others and can entrust ourselves to the omnipotence of love and our feeling of self-worth that it nourishes.

In the fifth energy center, the wonderful blue of the lapis lazuli supports our communication and our verbal expression. We perceive both the importance of communication and the idea that we can "talk something to death." Trust in the effectiveness of our words is created, and we learn to very consciously communicate and give our language wisdom and strength. The high beings of the luminous golden pyrite inclusions bear the sound and content of our words out into the world so that all those to whom we have something to say from the source of divine wisdom are guided to us.

In the sixth energy center, the lapis lazuli permeates the main energy stream of this center, which vibrates in dark-blue light. This greatly strengthens the trust in the divine guidance and wisdom can reveal itself in our daily life. Time and again, we are permitted to experience what it means to entrust oneself to this wise guidance. Our live transforms itself in this continually experiencable divine wisdom, which leads us to our weaknesses and shadow sides in order to let the weaknesses become strengths, the shadows change into light, and our abilities turn into gifts. Our self-limitations expand themselves, the "impossible" can become possible, and the things we would have never taken on before become reality and materialize.

In the seventh energy center, the deep blue of the lapis lazuli strengthens our belief in God and God's omnipresence. The searching of our soul and our turning to God becomes completely free of all doubts and can totally devote itself to the infinite silence. Peace comes into our being; the will of God and God's universal wisdom reaches us in this peace.

The lapis-lazuli Reiki (self-)treatment is a help in strengthening our power of faith and developing high intuition for sensitizing our perception of divine guidance and wisdom. When we doubt ourselves and our abilities time and again, when we don't know what we want, when we don't "rest" within ourselves, the dark blue of the lapis lazuli has a healing effect upon us.

When we place a tumbled lapis-lazuli stone on each energy center for Reiki treatment, our power of faith in all areas of our life is intensified.

With the lapis lazuli cut as a cabochon on each energy center, our conscious is filled with peace, stillness, and wisdom from the homeland of our soul. The highest divine perceptions can reveal themselves. The oval form lets us perceive the meaning of physical weakness, suffering, and illness, strengthening us with the power of faith for overcoming these limitations and imbalances.

The teardrop shape unites the soul's great power of faith with our divine purpose so that we increasing know what our purpose and the sense of our life is, learning to overcome all inhibiting fears and influences with trust in the divine guidance.

The round form rounds off our ideas and self-concepts and helps us give up (personal) resistance through insight into the great cosmic correlations.

The egg form lets us gain trust in the immeasurable divine wisdom time and again, helping us permit something new to reveal itself from the world of light through the increased sensitization of our consciousness, expressing its desire to be born on the earth.

A lapis lazuli-ball on each energy center strengthens and perfects our universal consciousness. There is nothing in our life that could shake our trust in God. We know about God's wise guidance and providence, recognize and respect the karmic laws of cause and effect, and learn to develop responsibility for our thoughts, feelings, and actions.

Seven Amethysts

Transformation, Dissolution of Karma, the Highest in Everything

When we put an amethyst on each energy center for the Reiki (self-)treatment, a violet stream flows through our energy systems and, pervaded with light, rises up with Reiki into the vibrations of the great cosmic color stream. Here it merges with the violet color stream and the light beings that are connected with the amethysts placed on our body. In the violet color stream, they come down to us with the highest color vibrations that our human eye can see and stimulate the highest quality within us on all levels. It is a transformational power that releases and frees us from dependencies and entanglements with matter and leads us to the fulfillment of our creative powers on a higher level. Our sensual/earthly passions are transformed into devotion to our divine tasks, to our calling.

Particularly the Reiki (self-)treatment with a grown, uncut amethyst tip on each energy center and between our feet activates the violet flame in our life stream, which "burns" karmic energy, redeeming and transforming it into divine grace. A great purification of the consciousness from abused powers that are not used in the divine sense frees us from the many feelings of guilt, the rigid blocks and the fears in life, the inner prohibitions, the coldness to ourselves and others, as well as illness and suffering manifested in our life.

110

The Amethyst in the Individual Energy Centers

In the first energy center, the violet light of the amethyst and its light beings help us to release the constantly recurring painful entanglements of karma with which we cause failures and great suffering on our existential, material, and physical plane and experience healing on the highest level of consciousness. Our drives are increasingly directed towards our higher task and no longer towards the increase of material gain and earthly pleasures.

In the second energy center, through the amethyst we experience deliverance from the frequently recurring difficulties in dealing with people with whom we live in a closer connection, whether the partnership be in the family, professional life, or our circle of friends. We find our way to a new encounter on higher levels, to a new attitude towards the "other" by recognizing and respecting the highest quality in the other person and not just seeing what causes us problems.

In the third energy center, the tendencies towards fear, mistrust, arrogance, a striving for dominance, helplessness, and an abuse of power are transformed into the ability of developing courage, trust, self-confidence, humbleness, responsibility, power, and strength. All of the forces within us unite in order to express the highest quality in our own way. We find deliverance from selfish and egocentric ways of behaving and objectives within this.

In the fourth energy center, the love of our heart is elevated by the violet of the amethyst so that we can develop our spirituality and devotion to the highest quality and decipher our holy mystery. Within this vibration, the highest truth that our soul has already achieved in previous lives flows into our consciousness and reveals to us further secrets of life and their beneficial application in our current existence.

In the fifth energy center, the amethyst's violet energy stream stimulates spiritual/mental communication, with which we learn to overcome the limitation of space and time. The highest quality within us communicates with the highest quality in others, independent of the other's personal presence and timeplan.

In the sixth energy center, the amethyst releases us from presumptuous, egocentric, power-oriented self-concepts and activates within us the highest intuition and spiritual contemplation, which leads us to consciously experienced unity with light-filled beings, their hierarchies, and tasks.

In the seventh energy center, the power of the amethyst streams into the main energy stream of this center, which is violet. In this activation, the mystery of divine reunification is performed at the highest step. In perfect devotion, we become free of our urge to want to experience the highest quality through our individual personality and can immerse ourselves as "nothing in nothing," experiencing the divine unity in everything.

The amethyst Reiki (self-)treatment is a great support when we long for the divine in our life, for transformation of our dependencies from material striving, for the dissolution of constantly recurring, oppressive experiences.

As already has been mentioned, the treatment using an uncut amethyst tip on each energy center and between the feet and with the tip pointed towards the head is very special. It activates the violet flame that frees us from karmic burdens and one-sided modes of behavior and attitudes, leading us to the divine and to our spiritual potential. This particularly helps people who "quarrel" with their fate, who are dissatisfied, who no longer see a meaning in their life, who are thirsty for power, and who harm themselves time and again without noticing the cause.

When we place a tumbled amethyst stone on each energy center, we will generally be supported in our need for a spiritual orientation, for transformation, for the raising of our consciousness.

With amethysts in the cabochon cut we strengthen our turn towards the highest quality in relation to our earthly existence. A cabochon in oval form on each energy center lets us overcome physical suffering by being able to perceive karmic correlations and freeing ourselves from them with spiritual help. The teardrop shape brings feelings into our consciousness with which we burden ourselves, which desire the experience of purification and seek an orientation towards divine unity.

Round cabochons support our mental world with the highest intuition and dissolve the structures in our thinking that cause harm. The square form helps us recognize our earthly dependencies and free ourselves of them.

When we put a faceted, cut amethyst on each energy center, activations take place that help us once again find God within our self. We can experience in many ways that God is not outside of us but lives within us and works through us.

The square form in a facet cut helps us live in harmony with the divine on earth and be connected with the highest quality in everything we do.

With the oval faceted, cut amethysts, we are very intensely permeated with healing power from the highest source. This sensitizes our consciousness for the correlations of our physical body with our subtle bodies and their response to vibrations from the surrounding world that have an oppressive or harmonizing effect. The faceted teardrop form touches the highest spiritual potential of our soul and supports us in expressing the experience of the divine within our personality.

With the round amethyst in the facet cut, we learn to apply the abilities and talents we have developed during the earthly life for unfolding and perfecting our spiritual gifts. Our spirituality is activated on the highest level with divine consciousness.

The Reiki (self-)treatment with an amethyst pyramid on each energy center is something special. This activates within us the development of highest spirituality and its manifestation in our earthly life. When we align the pyramids with one corner towards the head (cf. pg. 41), a concentrated violet light with the power of transformation in our earthly existence results. As a result, our life takes on a spiritual direction, our needs, longings, drives, and dependencies are transformed into the innermost freedom with which we enthusiastically develop our spiritual gifts and are allowed to accompany people in their process of inner transformation.

If we direct the pyramids with one side surface towards the head, the violet light flows upwards in a very concentrated form, for the further development of our spiritual wisdom and talent, for the transformation of our karmic burdens, and spiritual/mental powers that are abused, falsely directed, or have not yet been put to use.

Seven Quartz Crystals

Bringers of Light, Purity, Clarity, Purposefulness, Simplicity

When we put a quartz crystal on each energy center for the Reiki (self-)treatment, a pure light pervades us and rises up into the pure light of the universe through our active life stream. There it touches a level upon which the crystal light, the Christ energy, is manifest in a very special way around the earth in the "circle of crystals." Here each quartz crystal vibrates as a light crystal in the form in which it has grown on the earth or into which it has been cut, surrounded by its light beings. When our light stream arrives at the "circle of crystals" through the crystal Reiki (self-)treatment, this evokes a great luminance and radiance and calls the light beings of the crystal that accompanies us to the earth. They come as bringers of light and remind us of the original sea of eternal light, from which everything has been created and into which everything returns, and of the strong light power with which Christ has raised up the earth into the light.

The quartz crystals are manifestations of the light in which all the powers are still united in subtle vibrations and not divided into the color rays and their diversity. Their pure light connects not only with the bright light in our energy bodies and in our life stream, but also flows through all the color vibrations of our energy centers and the energy systems connected with them so that everything within us becomes brighter, lighter, and easier.

Whenever we long for purification, clarification, order, and purposefulness, the emanation of the crystal light, which comes into an even more brilliant and concentrated vibration through Reiki, is a wonderful experience. Through the gift of simplicity, it leads us to holistic harmony.

The Quartz Crystal in the Individual Energy Centers

In the first energy center, the quartz crystal brings its order of light into our quite everyday life. This order of light is full of harmony and does not always correspond with our idea of order. We become familiar with clarity as an ordering principle. As a result, everything that we had previously felt to be complicated, insurmountable, and difficult becomes more simple.

In the second energy center, the pure light energy of the quartz crystal helps us be able to cleanse our relationships and encounters with others of prejudices. This means that we don't get stuck on the shadow sides, what we don't like and causes us difficulties, from a one-sided perspective, but also recognize (and respect) the light-filled sides, the virtues, the beauty, and uniqueness of the other person.

In the third energy center, a harmonious emanation that is benevolent and yet purposeful, permitting us to recognize and do what is essential, develops in our personality with the quartz crystal and its light beings. We learn to assert ourselves and stand our ground when it is necessary to do so and not when we just want to prove ourselves and our power to others.

In the fourth energy center, the light of the quartz crystal cleanses our heart of falsely understood love (and charity), teaching us to have a "pure heart." We learn to be very "clear" with ourselves and others and not become too engrossed in our own feelings. In the innermost place of our heart center, the center of love, the crystal light touches the flame of the eternal light within us. This allows it to become a living, exuberant source of light that exudes its harmony in abundance and purity.

In the fifth energy center, the quartz crystal brings clarity into our verbal expression and helps us express "great things" in simplicity. As a result, with our communication we let harmony flow into a conversation, a room, our environment so that "dark," discordant, and oppressive vibrations and moods can be dissolved.

In the sixth energy center, the light of the quartz crystal purifies our thoughts, patterns of thinking, self-concepts, goals, and ideals of everything that does not lead us to the light. Our thinking becomes clear and ordered, and divine harmony guides our thoughts. Our intuition becomes permeated with light-consciousness so that we are more intensely connected with our Higher Self and all our helpers in the light.

In the seventh energy center, the crystal light comes into our highest vibrations, where it finds itself in the highest quality time and again. On the one hand, this has a relieving effect on the blocks with which we still orient our lives in too much of a manner towards the material world. On the other hand, we become increasingly able to take in the light from the highest source in perfect purity and simplicity, letting it have an effect within us and through us on the earth.

The quartz-crystal Reiki (self-)treatment leads us to a clear, purposeful way of living in all areas of our life. It helps us let our shadow sides come to the light and unite them with divine harmony. When we see our weaknesses in the light, they develop into strengths. This is so cleansing, relieving, strengthening, and light-filling for the body, soul, and mind that we should give (ourselves) this treatment on a regular basis.

The effect of the cleansing, clarity, and purposefulness is particularly strong when we place a grown, uncut quartz-crystal tip on each energy center with the tip pointing towards the head. A bright stream of light fills us and cleanses our body. Discordant, disease-causing, oppressive, and blocking energies can dissolve within this strong light stream and flow away in the light. Our level of emotions and thoughts also experience cleansing in this manner. A pleasant clarity remains with us, enabling us to tackle and solve difficulties, problems, and challenges in simplicity.

When we put a cut crystal tip with a base that has also been cut into a tip, so that the quartz crystal has two opposite tips, on each energy center, both a great deal of power of assertion and permeability develop simultaneously in the strong stream of light. Whatever has been hard and rigid, meaning the strongest of blocks, is broken though and brought back into a lively vibration at the same time. On the physical level, this is particularly helpful in cases of stiffening and paralysis.

When powers of assertion are lacking, energies are activated on the emotional level that help us be clear, purposeful, and full of initiative. Our world of thought can clearly orient itself towards the goal to be achieved, concentrating on it and creating a relationship to reality for its implementation.

With a quartz-crystal pyramid on each energy center, we manifest the light into the vibrations of this center. If we position each pyramid in such a way that a side surface points towards the head, so that a triangle points to the head (cf. pg. 41), a light pyramid develops within each energy center, making it possible for our consciousness to go beyond its earthy limitations in an enormous stream of light. It leaves the body, as well as the earth with its embodiments, as far as possible and temporarily returns to the temple of light that is familiar to our soul. This is usually a very strong experience, filling us with high light vibrations and initiating us into the mysteries of life in the light.

When we align the pyramids with one corner towards the head, strong healing powers flow out of the temples of light to our earth. These cleanse, organize, and strengthen our earthly life, lifting it up into the harmony of light. This healing is intensely oriented towards our body and strengthens us in the consciousness that the body is a vessel for the soul, through which it can exist here on earth. When this vessel is cleansed, it becomes a temple of light for the soul, making it possible for the divine light to live and shine on the earth.

The Reiki (self-)treatment with quartz-crystal pyramids on each energy center is very intensely effective and shouldn't be done too frequently, meaning not every day, at best just once a week. Greater intervals of time are even better. It helps us immerse ourselves in great experiences of light and increasingly turn towards the light in order to manifest and embody it upon the earth. This triggers extensive processes of purification and harmonization, as well as changes in our life that desire to be experienced, endured, and integrated.

While the crystals tips and pyramids support the purposefulness of quartz crystal, the forms described in the following tend to mitigate this through their more rounded cut, bringing more softness and harmony.

When we place a quartz-crystal tumbled stone on each energy center, we become faced with our weaknesses in order to honestly look at them with the clarity of the light and confront them. We stop making other people responsible for our difficulties and start working on ourselves.

When we give Reiki together with a quartz-crystal egg on each energy center, something new is animated within us through the crystal's stream of light. Not only are the thoughts, feelings, and ways of behaving purified, but the ordering power of the crystal light in the egg form brings us vibrations that help us allow a light-filled new beginning. The divine power of creation inspires us and supports a birth into the light.

A quartz-crystal ball on each energy center very strongly activates the cosmic consciousness within us. We are permitted to have an extensive look at the world of light and perceive everything necessary for the development of our light consciousness. With the form of the ball, the perfection of the light centers us and releases us from everything that is one-sided. We find our unity in the world of polarity and become the master of our life.

The Effects of Reiki Treatment with Gemstones

The effects of the Reiki (self-)treatments with the seven gemstones described here are usually not perceptible and visible after the first application. Instead, they require repeated stimulation so that the subtle energy can manifest and express itself in our coarse matter, in our body. There are exceptions where the strong impulse of Reiki with gemstones initiates a decisive turn of events and changes after just one (self-)treatment. However, Reiki and the light powers of the gemstones have much more to give us than the spontaneous healing of a physical symptom. These light-filled and loving universal life energies are here for holy healing, with which we can once again become connected with the light within us and within everything, consciously opening ourselves up to the loving emanation of this light. Our consciousness and therefore our attitude towards life and lifestyle will change when we turn to the light of the love of the universe time and again. We have become familiar with a very simple and natural possibility here with Reiki and gemstones which, if we ourselves are a Reiki channel, flows through us everyday by the laying on of hands, heightened with the luminous colors of the gemstones that we lay on for this purpose. Their light beings will permeate the life stream of our energy bodies, energy centers, and energy systems. This is a very special present to ourselves that we should give every day, if at all possible.

When we give Reiki with gemstones to a partner, it is helpful to tell him in a conversation beforehand that although his affliction—whether it is on the physical or the emotional level—has led him to us, a holistically oriented process of becoming whole is cautiously taking place. This is in harmony with the perception and changing of our disease-causing, weakening, extreme, uncontrolled and unconscious ways of behaving. This requires his willingness to take responsibility for himself, for the causes of his affliction, and learn to let go of the familiar things that have made him sick. He must accept the changes that led him to healing and harmony.

However, each human being determines himself how quickly he goes through his process of becoming whole and healed and changed, as well as what he must clarify and develop for himself as a result and how frequently he needs Reiki and the gemstones' powers of light for this purpose.

Reiki always leads us to the roots of our affliction and to developing our abilities that want to come to light. It helps us in the healing process to be more strongly connected with the light and its all-embracing, unconditional love that understands and forgives everything, developing our light-consciousness on earth.

In this process, the gemstones are "highlights" that provide peaks, that let our inner beauty and hidden talents and gifts shine and become visible, awakening lively joy within us.

When these two powers flow together, there is a heightening of the light vibration in which divine love can come to us and find itself reflected in the love of our hearts, streaming to us on earth.

We swim in a sea of grace
and yet, are often close to dying of thirst
because we do not drink from it.

(J. Kentenich)

The Author

Ursula Klinger-Omenka was born in 1950. After her academic education, she had intensive experiences and training in faith healing, esoteric psychology, reincarnation therapy, autogenous training, yoga, and meditation. On the path of her spiritual development, she encountered Reiki in 1983. She received the initiation into the First and Second Reiki Degrees, and ultimately the Reiki Master Degree in the traditional line of the Grand Master from Phyllis Lei Furumoto. In 1984, she was brought into contact with the subtle power powers of gemstones by a shaman.

Ursula Klinger-Omenka founded the Institute for Holistic Psychology in 1983 and now heads it together with her husband Ikechukwu Simeon Omenka, Reiki Master, in Nonnenhorn near Lindau, Germany (Lake Constance). In 1995, she established the association "Promotion of International Meeting Reiki-Nigeria" as a non-profit organization and established a Reiki clinic in Nigeria. Together, the couple gives individual sessions, initiations, advanced seminars and training in Reiki with gemstones, supported by the natural sounds of the drum and other instruments. In addition, they hold lectures and seminars in Germany and abroad.

Her books "The Secrets of Precious Stones", published by Lotus Light in 1988, pp128 and "Gemstone Power Meditation," (to be soon released by Lotus Light) are among the most popular English titles on this topic.

Paul Rudé

Souls to Soles

**A Self-Help Exploration
of Reflexology**

Caring for the feet has been part of
the culture of many civilizations, for
thousands of years. Now bursting
forth all over the world, reflexology
is being widely accepted as a safe,
powerful means of reducing stresses,
promoting vitality and well-being.
The author has masterfully captured
the essence of reflexology with beautiful illustrations and clearly presented guides for using your touch
effectively on the feet. Truly an exploration, this book takes you on a
fun loving adventure that has value
for all age groups. Breaking new
ground, this book also shows you
how to reach out to the young, to help
them in their times of discomfort, a
tender loving experience for those
who cannot help themselves.

160 pages, $12.95
ISBN 0-914955-51-9

Franz Benedikter

The Secrets of Loving Touch

**How the Loving Touch Releases
Hormones that Benefit Health,
Happiness, and Beauty and Are
Essential for Complete Physical
and Spiritual Well-Being**

Psychologist Franz Benedikter helps
readers create the best possible hor-
monal basis for a healthy, happy, and
liberated life. A release of relaxing,
activating, and euphoretic hormones
occurs when certain trigger zones of
the body are gently touched. With this
compact exercise program, we can
have a positive effect on the body,
mind, and soul through a form of self-
massage and partner massage that
is more like a loving touch. Since
every healthy person has a longing
to be touched, this book introduces
a new age of tenderness.

144 pages, 12.95 $
ISBN 0-941524-90-6

Walter Lübeck

Rainbow Reiki

**Expanding the Reiki System
with Powerful Spiritual Abilities**

Rainbow Reiki gives us a wealth of possibilities to achieve completely new and different things with Reiki than taught in the traditional system. Walter Lübeck has tested these new methods in practical application for years and teaches them in his courses.

Making Reiki Essences, performing guided aura and chakra work, connecting with existing power places and creating new personal ones, as well as developing Reiki Mandalas, are all a part of this system. This work is accompanied by plants devas, crystal teachers, angels of healing stones, and other beings of the spiritual world.

192 pages, $14.95
ISBN 0-914955-28-4

Walter Lübeck

Reiki—Way of the Heart

**The Reiki Path of Initiation
A Wonderful Method for Inner
Development and Holistic Healing**

Reiki—Way of the Heart is for everyone interested in the opportunities and experiences offered by this very popular esoteric path of perception, based on easily learned exercises conveyed by a Reiki Master to students in three degrees.

If you practice Reiki, the use of universal life energy to heal oneself and others, you will have the possibility of receiving direct knowledge about your personal development, health, and transformation.

Walter Lübeck also presents a good survey of various Reiki schools and shows how Reiki can be applied successfully in many areas of life.

192 pages, $ 14.95
ISBN 0-941524-91-4

Jutta Mattausch

Tibetan Power Yoga

**The Essence of All Yogas
A Tibetan Exercise for
Physical Vitality
and Mental Power**

Here is an absorbing story set in distant Tibet, and yet could also take place within all of us anywhere in the world, since it deals with the journey to the self. Whether you arrive at yourself and then perhaps also find yourself, depends on your willingness to open up ... This completely undogmatic book deals with one of the oldest exercises in the world, an exercise that is simple and unique. "The Tibetan Power Yoga" is what the Tibetan Lama Tsering Norbu calls this set of strong motions, similar to a "great wave" that has given the people from the Roof of the World physical vitality and mental power up into ripe old age since time immemorial.

112 pages, $9.95
ISBN 0-914955-30-6

Frank Arjava Petter

Reiki Fire

**New Information about
the Origins of the Reiki Power
A Complete Manual**

The origin of Reiki has come to be surrounded by many stories and myths. The author, a free Reiki master practicing in Japan, immerses it in a new light as he traces Usui-san's path back through time with openness and devotion. He meets Usui's descendants and climbs the holy mountain of his enlightenment. Reiki, shaped by Shintoism, is a Buddhist expression of Qigong, whereby Qigong depicts the teaching of life energy in its original sense. An excellent textbook, fresh and rousing in its spiritual perspective and an absolutely practical Reiki guide. The heart, the body, the mind, and the esoteric background, it is all here.

144 pages, $12.95
ISBN 0-914955-50-0

Rodolphe Balz

The Healing Power of Essential Oils

Fragrance Secrets for Everyday Use. This handbook is a compact reference work on the effects and applications of 248 essential oils for health, fitness, and well-being

Fifteen years of organic cultivation of spice plants and healing herbs in the French Provence have provided Rodolphe Balz with extensive knowledge about essential oils, how they work, and how to use them.

The heart of *The Healing Power of Essential Oils* is an essenial-oil index describing their properties, followed by a comprehensive therapeutic index for putting them to practical use. Further topics of this indispensible aromatherapy handbook are distillation processes, concentrations, chemotypes, quality and quality control, toxicity, self-medication, and the aromatogram.

208 pages, $ 14.95
ISBN 0-941524-89-2

Magie Tisserand · Monika Jünemann

The Magic and Power of Lavender

The Secret of the Blue Flower

The scent of lavender practically has permeated whole regions of Europe, contributing to their special character, and dominated perfumery for most of its history. To this very day, lavender has remained one of the most familiar, popular, and utilized of all fragrances.

This book introduces you to the delightful and enticing secrets of this plant and its essence, demonstrating its healing power, while also presenting the places and people involved in its cultivation. The authors have asked doctors, holistic health practitioners, chemists, and perfumers about their experiences and share them – together with their own with you.

136 pages, $ 9.95
ISBN 0-941524-88-4

Dr. Paula Horan

Empowerment Through Reiki

The Path to Personal and Global Transformation

In a gentle and loving manner, Dr. Paula Horan, world-renowned Reiki Master and bestselling author, offers a clear explanation of Reiki energy and its healing effects. This text is a must for the experienced practitioner. The reader is leaded through the history of this remarkable healing work to the practical application of it using simple exercises. We are not only given a deep understanding of the Reiki principles, but also an approach to this energy in combination with other basic healing like chakra balancing, massage, and work with tones, colors, and crystals. This handbook truly offers us personal transformation, so necessary for the global transformation at the turn of the millennium.

160 pages, $ 14.95
ISBN 0-941524-84-1

Dr. Paula Horan · Brigitte Ziegler M. A.

Dissolving Co-dependency

Powerful Insights from Core-Empowerment Training

Dr. Paula Horan, a noted American psychologist, and her partner Brigitte Ziegler, a well-known German seminar leader, are both Reiki Masters, well-versed in a wide variety of mind/body systems. They have put together a very powerful training program to assist people in the dissolution of a lifetime of inappropriate thought, emotional, and behavioral patterns. The ultimate necessity of "waking up" in its truest sense, gives very in-depth background to the real workings of the human mind. Each chapter is followed by a simple exercise to help the reader assimilate every area of understanding. This book is meant for people seeking greater knowledge about themselfs, with a sincere desire to get in touch with the core of their being.

104 pages, $ 9.95
ISBN 0-941524-86-8

Sources of Supply:

The following companies have an extensive selection of useful products and a long track-record of fulfillment. They have natural body care, aromatherapy, flower essences, crystals and tumbled stones, homeopathy, herbal products, vitamins and supplements, videos, books, audio tapes, candles, incense and bulk herbs, teas, massage tools and products and numerous alternative health items across a wide range of categories.

WHOLESALE:

Wholesale suppliers sell to stores and practitioners, not to individual consumers buying for their own personal use. Individual consumers should contact the RETAIL supplier listed below. Wholesale accounts should contact with business name, resale number or practitioner license in order to obtain a wholesale catalog and set up an account.

Lotus Light Enterprises, Inc.

P O Box 1008 RG
Silver Lake, WI 53170 USA
414 889 8501 (phone)
414 889 8591 (fax)
800 548 3824 (toll free order line)

RETAIL:

Retail suppliers provide products by mail order direct to consumers for their personal use. Stores or practitioners should contact the wholesale supplier listed above.

Internatural

33719 116th Street RG
Twin Lakes, WI 53181 USA
800 643 4221 (toll free order line)
414 889 8581 office phone
WEB SITE: www.internatural.com

Web site includes an extensive annotated catalog of more than 7000 products that can be ordered "on line" for your convenience 24 hours a day, 7 days a week.